Historic Neighborhoods of Baton Rouge

Historic NEIGHBORHOODS OF BATON ROUGE

Annabelle M. Armstrong

Charleston London

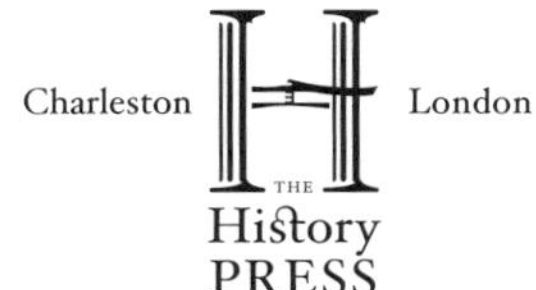

Published by The History Press
Charleston, SC 29403
www.historypress.net

Front cover, top center: Jeannette Thompson and her daughter, Andrea, enjoy the vintage free-standing swing, live oak and cistern, located on common ground near the entrance of Oakridge subdivision off Perkins Road. The developer, Sid Brian, donated the land to the Oakridge Civic Association.
Unless otherwise noted, all images are by the author.

First published 2010

Manufactured in the United States

ISBN 978.1.59629.839.2

Library of Congress Cataloging-in-Publication Data
Armstrong, Annabelle M.
Historic neighborhoods of Baton Rouge / Annabelle M. Armstrong.
p. cm.
ISBN 978-1-59629-839-2
1. Historic districts--Lousiana--Baton Rouge--Tours. 2. Baton Rouge (La.)--Tours. 3. Baton Rouge (La.)--Description and travel. 4. Baton Rouge (La.)--History. I. Title.
F379.B33A76 2010
976.3'18--dc22
2010026592

Contents

Contents

Contents

Introduction

Baton Rouge has a neighborliness unparalleled, a fact that I discovered quite incidentally, as a career journalist. Localites know that "Our Town" is a large river port, a state capital rich in history and famous for its food, politics, music and universities. Discovered in 1699 by the French Canadian explorer Pierre LeMoyne, Sieur D'Iberville, Baton Rouge (French for "red stick") was incorporated as a town in 1817 and, having flown under ten flags—more than any other city—possesses a magnetic multicultural aura.

Writing for a community newspaper, the *South Baton Rouge Journal*, I was asked to tell the story of Capital Heights subdivision. Young families were moving into the mid-city area, buying and refurbishing rundown shotgun-style houses, and had organized a civic association together with established occupants. Crime was down; property values were up.

I was a friend of the late Lerlind Hanchey and Violet May Stone, the daughters of Charles Roseman, who founded Capital Heights in 1918. After interviewing Violet May Stone, since deceased, I drove through Capital Heights to delight in homey, freshly painted houses and picket fences, carefully groomed lawns and leisurely bikers and walkers. Making inquiries of strangers, I was led to the president of the civic association, who gave me contacts and told me what the organization was doing to improve its quality of life. My bonus was to hear some grand stories of the past.

The readers wanted more. My wanderings through historic South Baton Rouge began. I was welcomed into countless hospitable homes from the

Garden District and eastward to the Airline Highway, the demarcation line for South and Southeast Baton Rouge, and all along historic Highland and Perkins Roads.

The city's early growth was an expansion of downtown near the Mississippi River, with Roseland Terrace in the Garden District its third subdivision, starting with Spanish Town in 1805. Today, Our Town is a metropolis, its population an estimated 809,282 in the Greater Baton Rouge area and 428,360 in the city limits (according to the Baton Rouge Area Chamber on May 7, 2010).

When I wrapped up the series in 2003, I had interviewed residents in sixty neighborhoods. I am glad that I chronicled these memories, because many who shared stories with me are now deceased, and others have relocated. I wrote each story according to the area covered by its civic or homeowners' association, in some cases one subdivision only, in others, several. Every area has a civic organization; the majority provides security patrols and sponsor regular social activities. Within these areas, neighbors do more than wave to one another. They care and work together, as the family they are.

Town by the River Starts Moving Out

The Garden District Still Blossoming

The historic Garden District has charm and character, with a cosmopolitan blend of residents and architectural styles. Composed of subdivisions Roseland Terrace (founded in 1911), Drehr Place (1919) and Kleinert Terrace (1925), the district attracts those who do not want to be like everyone else. David Madden, author-in-residence and LSU professor, described its "interesting characters" once in the neighborhood newsletter—and included himself.

When Roseland Terrace was established, it became the city's third subdivision, following Spanish Town (first laid out in 1805) and Beauregard Town (1806), both sited in the downtown area near the Mississippi River. (Much has been written about these initial subdivisions.) A pre–Civil War racetrack once stood on the site, and the Sixth Michigan Regiment camped here after Union forces captured Baton Rouge in 1862. The first baby born in Roseland Terrace was named Terrace Verbois.

Anne Marks helped research Roseland Terrace, classified as a Historic District on the National Register of Historic Places. (The city population in 1910 was 14,897.) Patricia Duncan, architectural historian, did the major research that helped classify Drehr Place and Kleinert Terrace as Historic Districts on the National Register. The district boundaries extend from Government Street on the north to Broussard Street/Magnolia Drive on

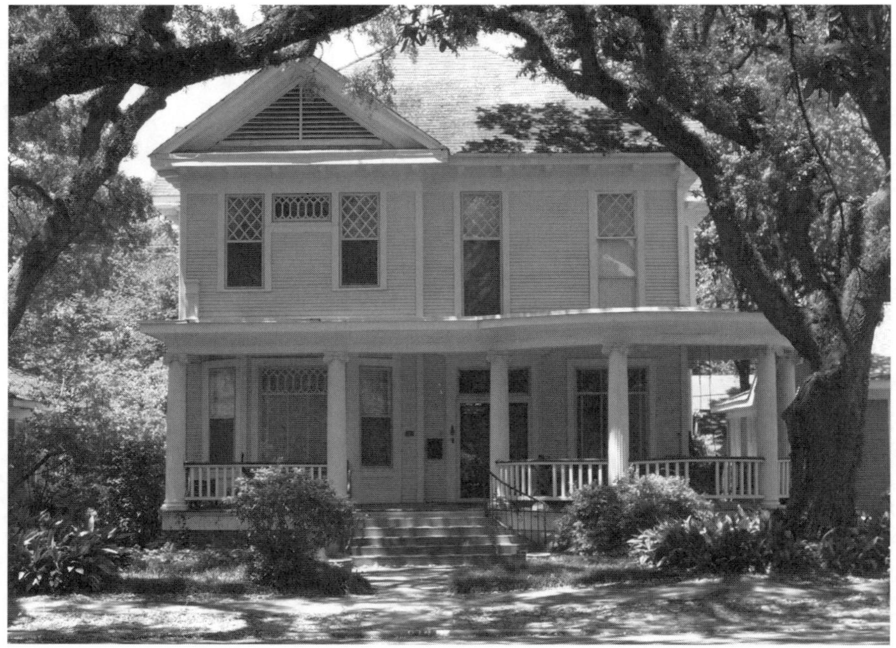

This 1912 Free Classic Queen Anne home at 614 Park Boulevard was one of the first built in the Garden District. *Photo by Kenny Armstrong.*

the south and South Eighteenth on the west to St. Rose on the east, with a section of Kleinert Terrace extending from South Eugene starting at Myrtle Street. Architectural styles include Italian Renaissance, Victorian, Colonial Revival and Tudor Revival, international-style and bungalows.

Although it covers thirty-eight blocks and includes more than eight hundred families, the Garden District has a bonded appeal. Longtime residents recalled when friends and neighbors of octogenarian Orion Hupperich, known as the "Bengal Bard," painted his house for him. A media favorite, the colorful Hupperich traveled by bicycle and largely spoke in rhyme.

"We're almost like pioneers," said four-time president of the civic association Flo Ulmer, describing neighbors who pride themselves on independent perspectives. She and her husband, videographer Bill Rodman, renovated a 1922 Norwegian cottage on Oleander Street. Across from them is the family of David Norwood, illustrator and preservationist. Norwood said, "I knew I'd like Dr. Frederick Billings the first time I saw him. He was in his front yard right on the boulevard [Kleinert Avenue] splashing around in a kiddie pool."

It is a place for surprises, particularly when homeowners start renovating and discover pegged nails in the floor or wiring from a former gambling operation.

Approximately three hundred homes are listed on the National Register, with more than fifty on Park Boulevard in Roseland Terrace, including the Reiley-Reeves house, the home of John S. "Chip" and Jane Coulter, 1910–11.

The Garden District's palatial touches include guesthouses, pools, basements (rare in the area) and a cupola. Home tours have been held as fundraisers on several occasions. Individual owners point out special features. For instance, Earl and Evelyne Francis like their 1929 Tudor Revival house with twelve-and-a-half-foot ceilings, ornate chimneys, basement, eight gables, eight outside arches and sixteen interior arches. They were told that its builder, Leslie Pecue, a millionaire and renowned gambler, imported some materials from Europe.

Mary Elizabeth Norckauer, former Louisiana State University (LSU) great athlete, said that her house on Camelia Avenue was built in the 1920s. "When my parents moved here in 1930 my father renovated it," she said. "There were empty lots and pastures on Kleinert and Terrace Avenues."

Generational ties are rampant, and increasing, across the Garden District. Attorney Sid Blitzer has lived with his wife, Carol Anne, on Myrtle Avenue since 1980 but grew up on Terrace Street, where his parents and maternal grandparents, Josh and Florence Kantrow, lived. Lewis Doherty IV became the third generation of Dohertys to live on Cherokee Street when he occupied a garage apartment behind the house where his father, Judge Lewis Doherty III, and uncle Anthony grew up. "The lot was given as a wedding present from my grandfather, William Doherty, to my parents, who built the house in 1925," said Doherty, retired judge. "Mother lived there seventy-two years until she died in 1997. I lived there until I married Arden in 1956. We had three drugstores nearby, McArthur's, Foss's and Griffon's. Arden and I could get a full meal for seventy-five cents at Griffon's, that also had a soda fountain."

Jesse Coates Jr. and his sister, Judy Dorfi of New Orleans, grew up on Terrace at Drehr. An LSU classroom, Charles E. Coates Hall, was named for his grandfather and Jesse Coates Hall, the LSU chemical engineering building, for his father. His wife, Ferrill Ann, who grew up on Park Boulevard, is a landscape architect who drew plans for a community garden and monitors the trees. He remembered riding bikes downtown. "All the neighborhood kids went to the movies on Saturday. We had four theaters in the late 1940s and 1950s: the Hart, the Paramount, the Louisiana and the Gordon." He walked to South Eugene and, at the end of Terrace, saw only pastures and horses. His father and T.W. Walsh built a baseball diamond for the children on Broussard Street.

Laura Walsh, widowed, said that she and her husband built their home on Broussard Street in January 1940. Her son, Allen, resides with his wife, Ruby Ann, and three children on Drehr Avenue in the home of the late Dr. Ashton Robins. The Robins house was the last private polling place in Baton Rouge.

Scenes from the movie *Lush*, starring George C. Scott Jr., were filmed at the Norwood home and the Lewis Gottlieb home, which has an elevator and swimming pool, on Drehr Avenue at Oleander Street.

A role model for civic associations, the Garden District networks with other community groups, sponsors social events, oversees safety, maintains boulevard medians, monitors the trees and updates signs and its properties with the city-parish.

WHERE NEIGHBORS ARE FAMILY: BROUSSARD

Across South Eugene Street from the Garden District is an upscale neighborhood of beautiful, commodious houses. The Broussard area was developed about thirty years after Roseland Terrace. However, St. Joseph's Academy moved from downtown and was built in 1941.

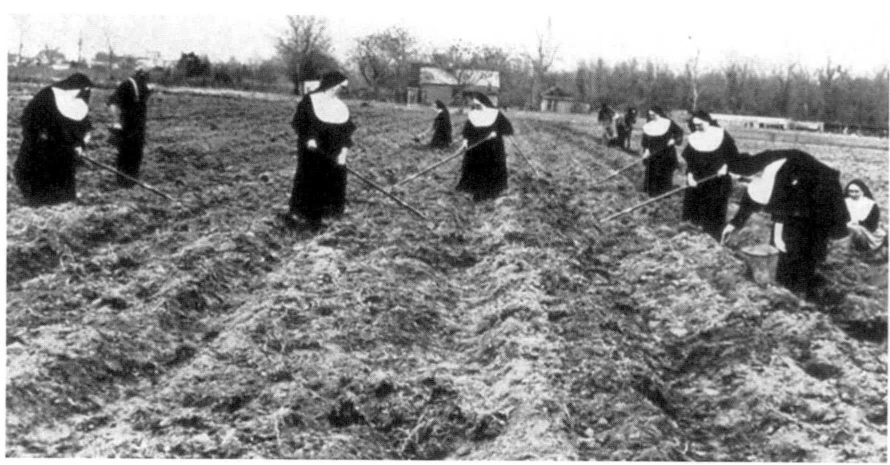

The Sisters of the Congregation of St. Joseph of Medaille hoed their Victory Garden at St. Joseph's Academy in 1944. *Courtesy of SJA.*

"When we built here in 1952, we were outside the city limits and the city bus stopped at Eugene Street," said Frank Bologna on Kleinert Avenue. "It was all fields around here, except for the academy across the street. Kleinert was a gravel road. We were one of three houses going up. The only house near us was that frame house across the street." He pointed to the 1935 home of Zed and Rachel Howell. The Bolognas' neighbors were his cousin, Antonio Joseph Bologna, and his wife, Margaret Ragusa Bologna.

After a stint in the U.S. Army, Frank began working with his father and uncle in the local Bologna Brothers business, purchased by the brothers in 1925. He married Maria Palermo of New Orleans in 1948. Four of their children live within four and a half blocks of them: Sandra Ribes, Phyllis Kerr, Eugene Bologna and Re DiVincenti. Son Paul lives in Woodchase subdivision.

DiVincenti and Patrice Ellis formed the Broussard Civic Association in 1986. "We have quite a few families whose backyards meet," DiVincenti said. Her family on Myrtle Avenue has a backyard that meets that of her parents.

Boundaries are South Eugene to the east, Parker Street to the west, Claycut Road to the north and Hundred Oaks Avenue to the south. "We govern three subdivisions: Marwede Place, McIver Place and Eastland Place," said DiVincenti. "We included Catholic High School, built in 1957, B'nai Israel Synagogue, 1954, and the academy." All three relocated from downtown. Catholic High began as St. Vincent's Academy in 1894, and B'nai Israel began in 1858.

"David and I built in 1979 on a lot we bought from my grandfather Eugene," she added. "We found horseshoes in the ground when we were digging. We built our two-story brick house with an open courtyard to look like New Orleans. I decided if I couldn't live in New Orleans, I would do the next best thing."

Association co-founder Patrice Ellis and her husband, Richard, bought their English cottage at the corner of Kenmore Avenue and Broussard Street in 1978. Interior designers, they went to work tearing down walls, making rooms and finishing the upstairs. "We closed off a hall and made a pantry, turned a staircase around, put decks in the back and have a heatilator so that we sit outside on a cold night and enjoy the deck," said Patrice.

Across the way is the academy, a fifteen-acre complex of seven buildings between Kleinert Avenue and Broussard Street. According to Sister Jean Fryoux, who taught fifty-six years before retiring, the Congregation of St. Joseph of Medaille sent four sisters from France to the area to help orphans.

In 1868, a school was opened on Church Street downtown (now Fourth Street) at Florida Street, and in 1890, a three-story school was built on that site. Two angel sculptures were moved from downtown to the current site.

Fryoux grew up in Baton Rouge and finished her schooling at the downtown academy in 1938. After studying at Loyola University and teaching in New Orleans, she returned to the academy in 1944 at its present location. "I remember when we lived downtown and had to ride the city bus. It stopped at Eugene, and we walked to Broussard," she said. "When we built the academy, we had a cafeteria in the back and toward Parker, and a pig pen, where we raised and sold pigs. There were no houses out here. Broussard was gravel, but once the school got here, it was blacktopped.

"In 1944, everyone had a Victory Garden. A neighbor with a mule plowed it, and we planted it." She watched each building being constructed and implemented this into her classroom lessons. "I was teaching the speed of sound while houses were going up across the street on Broussard. It worked out fine, as the students could watch and then hear the hammers strike."

Between Broussard and Hundred Oaks Avenues is the rolling terrain of Eastland Place. Dr. Joe MacCurdy said:

> *My uncle, Lowry Eastland, developed Eastland Place about 1949 and named several streets for neighbors, including Dr. C.C. Moreland and Buck Gladden. Uncle Lowry was from Oklahoma City and served in the U.S. Navy during World War I. After the war, he was on a train going home to Biloxi, heard someone talk about Baton Rouge, got off and stayed. He was successful in insurance and real estate. The biggest thing he did was buy three hundred acres on Jefferson Highway for about $49,000, which his widow Ernestine sold. This became Westminster, Jefferson Terrace and Pine Park.*

A Premier Attraction Near City Park

Restful and scenic, the McCall Place and City Park area is a favorite place for runners and bikers. Adjacent to the man-made lake overlooking City Park, developed in 1928, its magnetic beauty is enhanced by spreading live oaks planted by the late Steele Burden. McCall Place, with entrances off Perkins Road onto East Lakeshore Drive and Blouin Avenue, was developed in 1927.

"When my father developed McCall Place, it was rural property and Baton Rouge was a small town," said retired realtor Robert "Sonny"

Babington McCall Jr. "After LSU was moved from the state capitol area to its current site, the town started extending in this direction, following the Garden District and Roseland Terrace."

McCall Place runs between Perkins Road, from Blouin Avenue and East Lakeshore Drive to the railroad tracks. Two short streets extending between these two are named Robert and Eola after Robert McCall Sr. and his wife, Eola Blouin. McCall Jr. remembered when Perkins Swamp was being cleaned out and the lake developed from 1925 to 1928.

"Among the earliest residents to buy lots and build were Dr. Irving Foote Jr., an LSU professor, who bought the first lots on Blouin Avenue," he said. "Dr. Charles A. Jolly, a pharmacist, built the first house on East Lakeshore facing the golf course in 1929."

McCall's daughter, Julia McCall Hightower, shared a childhood memory of walking from her family home in Kleinert Terrace to City Park to rent skates. Longtime residents also recall the popular carousel.

At age eight, Joe Oubre hunted squirrels in Perkins Swamp before it was a lake. Oubre moved with his family from Mississippi to Baton Rouge in 1919 when he was six. "City Park was the second park in town. The first was Victory Park, a big park with a pool, between Laurel and Main Streets, near the present-day interstate." Standing on his front lawn on East Lakeshore Drive, surveying rolling hills and native trees, he asked, "Where else would you have a view like this? We have a thirty-five-foot drop from Perkins Road on high land to the lake."

His wife, Dot Oubre, grew up on North Boulevard near the Old Governor's Mansion. George W. Garig was commissioner of streets and parks, responsible for the development of the lake and golf course. "When I was a little girl, the Garigs lived next door; his wife, Aminie, was my godmother," said Dot. "Mr. Garig had one of the first automobiles in Baton Rouge—red, with no top on it. He loved to ride me around. One day he said, 'My girl, someday this swamp will be a lake.' I was in preschool when the lake and golf course were developed."

The first house that eminent architect A. Hays Town designed in Baton Rouge, after he moved his family here in 1939, is located at 1611 East Lakeshore Drive. The 2,500-square-foot brick house was built for the Elbert E. Moore of Louisiana National Bank. Its classic touches include the columned front porch, louvered windows, foyer and arched entrance to the living room.

In 1974, George and Lillie Petit Gallagher made their home in a two-story circa 1937 house on East Lakeshore Drive. Lillie, a historian, said that Bunkie banker Leonard Caldwell built the house for his family because he wanted them to have a Baton Rouge home while his children attended LSU. He used tall virgin timber, with the thirty-six-foot depth of the main house from front-to-back windows determined by the length of the pine and cypress beams. The Gallaghers converted a sunroom, added by prior residents Governor and Mrs. Robert Kennon, into a reading room. Lillie also spearheaded community action to preserve the historic City Park Golf Course, laid out in 1927 by Tom Bendalow, a noted Scottish golf course designer.

Attorneys Jules and Frances Landry moved to Lake Hills Parkway in 1950. Their white brick house on four lots is entered from Lakeshore, where a classic, columned garage adds a touch of formal antiquity. Preservationists, the couple restored the Lafayette Building, said to be the city's oldest commercial structure, built in mid-eighteenth century, on Lafayette Street. Their next-door neighbors, Francis and Jessie Ellender Henchy, who have occupied a 1937 stucco hilltop house since 1955, watched five children grow up golfing and swimming at City Park. "Our youngest son, John, was BREC city champion senior golfer three times," said Jessie.

Neighbors in close-by Lake Hills subdivision, developed in 1927, formed an association in the 1990s and joined efforts with the McCall Place/City Park. One access point is located off East Lakeshore onto Lake Hills Parkway. City Park Realty, with Clive Kernan as president, was the developer.

In 1948, adjacent Hillsdale was developed, and its civic association—created by attorneys Warren O. Watson, Fred Blanche and Mack H. Hornbeak—remains active. Hillsdale residents also take part in the City Park Patrol, founded by policeman Dennis Smith and Julie Gremillion in 1996.

In 1965, Warren Watson Jr. built a brick hilltop house on Cottonwood Avenue for his family; after his death in 1982, his widow, Ann, remarried and, with her husband David Hedgepeth, remained there. Ann said, "We have seen children grow up here, marry and move back. And for years we have loved to grocery shop at Bet-R and Bolton's Drug Store."

A Plantation Called Hundred Oaks

The fascinating history of the aptly named Hundred Oaks area is one of plantations and Civil War stories, followed by dairy farms and the Perkins Road Overpass. Before the Civil War, it was Richland Plantation and, later,

Perkins Grove, Bonnie Grove and, finally, Hundred Oaks Plantation. The latter was 2,800 acres of sugar cane. Twin brothers Dr. Henry and Dr. John "Jehu" Perkins, from a wealthy Kentucky family, brought their brides with them during the early part of the nineteenth century and established what was said to be the largest plantation east of the Mississippi at one time. Their showplace three-story home had a frontal colonnade of great columns, interior marble stairs and a tropical roof garden. Horse and carriage entered through gates at the Perkins Road end of Reymond Avenue that led to the home on Parker at the other end.

Today in Hundred Oaks Park, developed in 1927 by Samuel Isaac Reymond, Miles and Mary Pollard live on the site of the 1808 Hundred Oaks Plantation home. Their house was built in 1937 by Yola Cohn, who, after being widowed, married Marion Kahn. She built the house next door for her son, Henry Louis Cohn Jr., today the home of Dr. Carl and Diane Luikart.

According to Jack Reymond Whitaker, great-nephew of S.I. Reymond, the plantation home was heavily damaged by shells in the Civil War and, at one time, was a hospital. Reymond lived in the remaining wing until the onset of the Great Depression. "These were tough times," said Whitaker. "My grandmother, Anna Reymond Whitaker, lended S.I., her brother, $8,000. When he defaulted in 1932, she took over and moved my parents, sister and me into the house. I was ten years old."

Whitaker recalled watching Kansas City Southern steam locomotives whiz down the tracks. "I had a clear view, with no trees or overpass, and could see clearly to Perkins Road," he said.

Anna Whitaker sold the plantation house to Yola Kahn for $10,000. Whitaker said his great-uncle "lost everything, including Reymond's Department Store on Third Street in the Reymond Building." He added that before the crash, his uncle had already developed his 'country' subdivision. Later, after moving from the plantation home, he took scrap lumber and built a house on a hill that later became the site of the Daggett home, which was located in what is now Eliza Beaumont Lane area.

The Pollards' land retains some architectural annexes of the old plantation, such as the silos from S.I. Reymond's dairy. Yola Kahn cut off the tops, roofed them and used them for bathhouses for the swimming pool and guesthouses.

Along Reymond, a wide boulevard, residents plant and maintain the median. Architect Town put his stamp all along Reymond. At the foot of the Perkins Road Overpass is the stately, columned home of the Norman

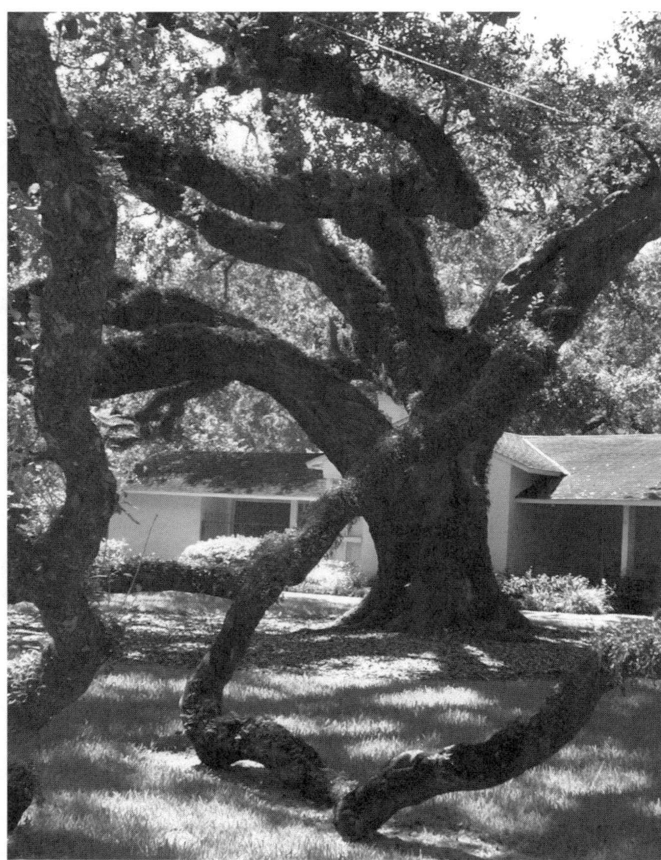

This breathtaking 280-year-old live oak on Reymond Avenue has had national recognition. *Courtesy of Cary Saurage.*

Saurage Jr. family, who own Community Coffee Company, founded by the senior "Cap" Saurage. It is fronted by a spectacular live oak tree, estimated at 280 years old and recognized by the nonprofit Cultural Landscape Foundation in Washington, D.C. Also on Reymond, an early house is the Mediterranean-style home of Sean and Jennifer Reilly, community activists, who have renovated it for their growing family. During construction, hundreds of dairy bottles from Hundred Oaks Dairy were unearthed.

Town also designed the hilltop home of Charles and Carol Lamar at Eugene and Tyrone, built for the late Dr. Thomas Y. Gladney, a physician and Golden Deeds Award winner. The civic association dedicated a triangular memorial garden at this juncture to his memory, with a marble marker of dedication.

The Hundred Oaks Civic Association also includes Zeeland Place (1928). Boundaries covered are Hundred Oaks to the north, Honeysuckle Street to the south, Parker Street to the east and the railroad tracks and Perkins on the west.

Diversified architecture extends from cottage to colonial-style, with numerous homes built in the late 1920s and 1930s. For example, at the corner of Lydia and Arlington is a 1921 brick house built for Sterling "Buck" Gladden Sr. His daughter-in-law, Marilyn Gladden, said the lumber for it was shipped on a boxcar by train from Bossier Parish and sat on the tracks on Perkins Road.

Lifelong resident Harold Bahlinger on Edward Avenue, who grew up at his late parents' home next door, recalled collecting greenback turtles in Dawson Creek and selling them for a nickel apiece at Sacred Heart Elementary School. He, his brother Julius, Jack Whitaker and George Simon Jr. were among the children who skateboarded down the hill at the corner of Arlington and Edward, a Spanish-style house then owned by Dr. and Mrs. Clarence Chamberlin.

Bahlinger said that another area dairy belonged to Thomas Dutsch, who delivered milk to the neighborhood first thing every morning. Julius Bahlinger said that they learned how to milk cows on the property that now belongs to the Catholic Diocese of Baton Rouge.

Here, all ages mingle in restaurants, at Perks Coffeehouse and at family-oriented businesses. The active civic association sponsors socials, including an annual picnic and Christmas party. It also has security fees and patrol and a newsletter, delivered by street captains.

Exclusive Eliza Beaumont Lane

At the end of Daggett Avenue in Hundred Oaks is a pocket subdivision, designed and developed by Mike Waller. He bought eight acres from the late Devan Daggett in 1976 and, by 1980, had completed the streets and built the first town house. "I patterned it after the New Orleans Garden District but was actually practicing New Urbanism and didn't know it," said Waller. Its gates are entered on Daggett Avenue, named for the first female law professor at LSU, Harriet Daggett, who lived on a hill overlooking the area before the construction of South Acadian Thruway.

The economy failed in 1987, and Waller never finished his dream development. The style had been set, though, and Eliza Beaumont Lane received an award from the Baton Rouge Growth Coalition in 2001.

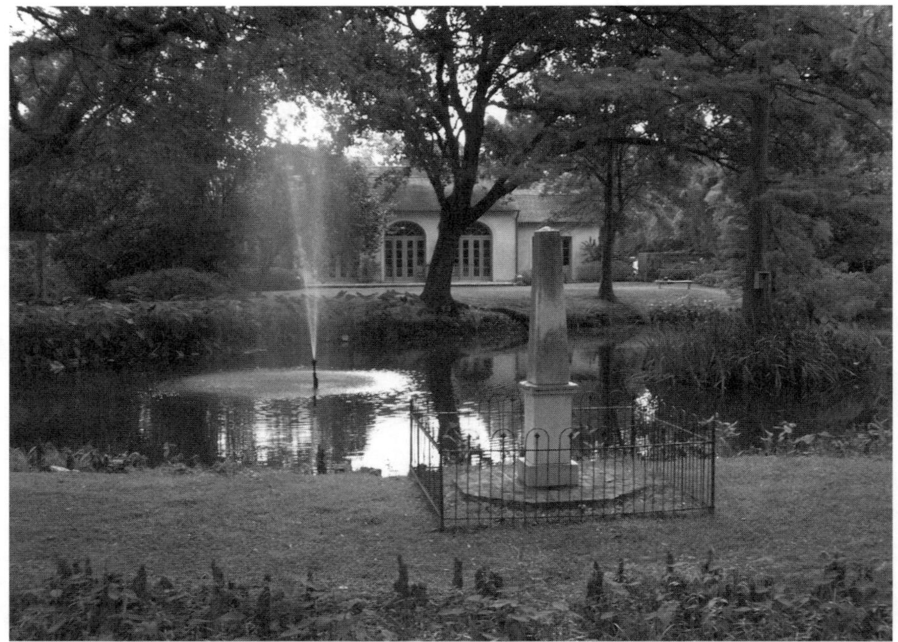

Touched by a nineteenth-century tragedy, Eliza Beaumont Lane developer Mike Waller relocated mother-daughter grave sites to an island pond.

In researching the monument just inside the gates, Waller discovered the tragic story of Dr. Thomas Beaumont. After being ridiculed by New Orleans physicians because he believed mosquitoes carried malaria—later found to be true—Beaumont moved to Baton Rouge in 1847. His twenty-two-year-old wife, Eliza, and thirteen-month-old daughter, Sarah, died shortly thereafter of malaria. Eventually, Beaumont became a colonel in the Confederate army and died in Tennessee. Waller moved the monument for Beaumont's wife and child from an unrecorded graveyard on the old plantation property, placed it on an island in the pond and enclosed it with a wrought-iron fence.

The lane curves into a combination of some twenty houses and town homes in such designs as American Creole, Victorian Creole and Federal American. Four homes, two on each side, front the lake. The first home to the right is occupied by attorney Gordon and Camilla Pugh, who first bought the L-shaped lot and then built the 4,450-square-foot home. Gordon said the idea for the front windows came from the Faculty Club at LSU. Three sets of arched French doors bring the outdoors into the living room and study. The Parisian bench by the pond was a gift to Gordon from his wife.

Freestanding houses across from the town homes include one of Linda Landry, early resident. "Only two houses were here when my house was built," she said. "We used the whole pond area and the hill for my daughter's wedding reception." Widowed in 1977 when her husband died at age forty-five, she designed the Acadian-style brick and stucco house with a front porch.

Waller designed and called the brick home of Lou and Gordon Ellis a "Hays Town Vernacular." Gordon Ellis said that "the morning sun coming through the trees across the lake is stunning."

This private community in the heart of a city has a New Orleans flavor and sense of history. Residents commented on the convenient location and have their own homeowners' association but also participate in the Hundred Oaks Association.

Expanding Eastward into the Countryside

The Resurgence of Capital Heights

When developed in 1918 by lumberman and real estate developer Charles Roseman, Capital Heights subdivision was considered "out in the country," said Violet May Stone, daughter of the late Roseman, who came to Baton Rouge in 1890. From her home in Roseman Place (1912), a small development near the Westmoreland Piccadilly, she recalled that Government Street was gravel with ditches on either side. "We used to go crawfishing in the ditches," she said. "There was a drainage culvert underneath Government. Mama would tell us to jump in the culvert if we heard a car coming so that no one would see us."

Stone rejoiced in the uplift of Capital Heights, bordered on the west by Acadian Thruway, on the east by Jefferson Highway, on the north by Government Street and on the south by Claycut Road.

In one of the city's oldest subdivisions, an influx of young families give new life to old houses. Through a proactive, strong civic association formed in 1992, the turnabout has brought an increase in property values and decrease in crime. Sparkling picket fences and freshly painted homes have visual appeal. Elderly gardeners and children at play comingle.

Capital Heights has 780 households. While many lots are forty feet wide with two-bedroom, one-bath homes, there are still imposing large

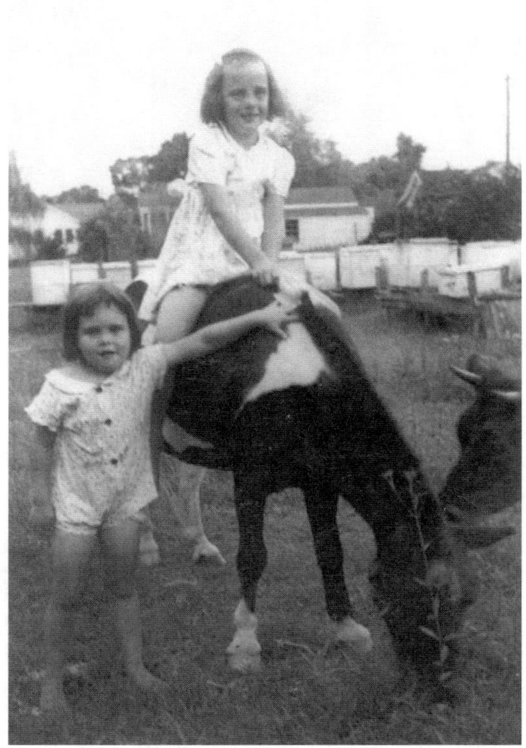

In 1945, June Blush (May), *standing left*, and Barbara Blush (Dodge) lived on Vernon Street (South Foster Drive). Beehives, background. *Courtesy of June May.*

properties, like the two-story antebellum home of Richard and Victoria "Tori" Preis on Claycut Road. "Our son Max is the fourth generation of my family to live here," Tori said.

Ned Clark, a retired banker who has lived on Moore Street since he was four, treasures the subdivision plats given to him by Stone. He and his wife, Laura, a realtor, have a daughter, Chrissie, who bought a cottage-style house on Claycut after a six-year search in the area. She said the ten-foot ceilings and room sizes in her circa 1930 home make the 1,400-square-foot home appear more spacious than it is. She relishes its hardwood floors, built-in bookshelves by the fireplace and kitchen china cabinet.

"When I moved here twenty-seven years ago, many of the original families were still here," said Joyce LeBlanc. "As they matured and moved away, there was a question of which way the neighborhood might go. The vitality of the young families ensures we are a viable community. I was a young chick when I moved here, and now I'm the old lady of the neighborhood."

LeBlanc's two-story 1938 home has a glassed-in sunroom, abounding with plant life. Here she can see the outside garden. "See those people walking by?" she asked. "I recognize many and also meet new people since I enjoy gardening and being out in my yard." She added, "Many modest houses are enhanced by the surrounding urban forest."

The area abounds with renovations, including a major undertaking of Craig and Yolanda Rabalais on Bienville Street. They purchased a two-story house in deplorable shape at a sheriff's sale for $45,000 and contributed $30,000 of materials, and Craig worked twelve hours on days off. The appraisal now exceeds $300,000.

George and Lucy Kadair reared eight children in their Wiltz Street home, where they resided fifty years, while Irma and Justin Smith reared four children, adding on to their house as needed. "We wouldn't be anywhere else for convenience," said Irma.

Steele Place and "Captain Ollie Steele"

Once part of Richland Plantation, owned by Captain Oliver Brice "Ollie" Steele, who fought with the Kentucky infantry during the Civil War, Steele Place is home to many prominent citizens. A pecan grove and plantation before its development, it retains its wide boulevards and large lots, many still an arpent (little less than an acre), as on the original subdivision map on October 2, 1923.

Captain Steele was a Confederate hero who entered the Civil War as a drummer boy and emerged as a captain of the famed Kentucky "Orphan Brigade." When the Union forces took Kentucky, his brigade could not go home, hence the label "orphan brigade." He relocated his family to his cotton plantation in north Louisiana near Monroe. Encouraged to run for political office, in 1885 he brought his family to Baton Rouge on a Mississippi riverboat, the *St. John*. He served as state auditor from 1904 to 1908 and state treasurer from 1908 to 1912.

Developed by Anthony F. "Tony" Cazedessus, Steele Place is bounded by Claycut Road and Hundred Oaks Avenue, also by Westmoreland Avenue and the west side of Glenmore Avenue. A copy of the original sales brochure, owned by attorney Jayne Middleton, includes a map citing Topic Street (now Westmoreland) and Cleon Street, which later became a portion of South Acadian Thruway. It states: "Steele Place is less than one mile from the city limits of Baton Rouge, on the Clay Cut Road, in view of the proposed City Park and joins Zeeland Place on the east."

At its Claycut Road entrance, Steele Place has four towering brick and concrete ornamental pillars. "August Ledoux, a brick mason, built the columns," said Sanders Cazedessus, retired attorney at home on Steele Boulevard with his wife, Morena. Their two-story antebellum house was built in 1975 on a lot purchased from Ione Easter Burden by Cazedessus and his late wife, Barbara Walters.

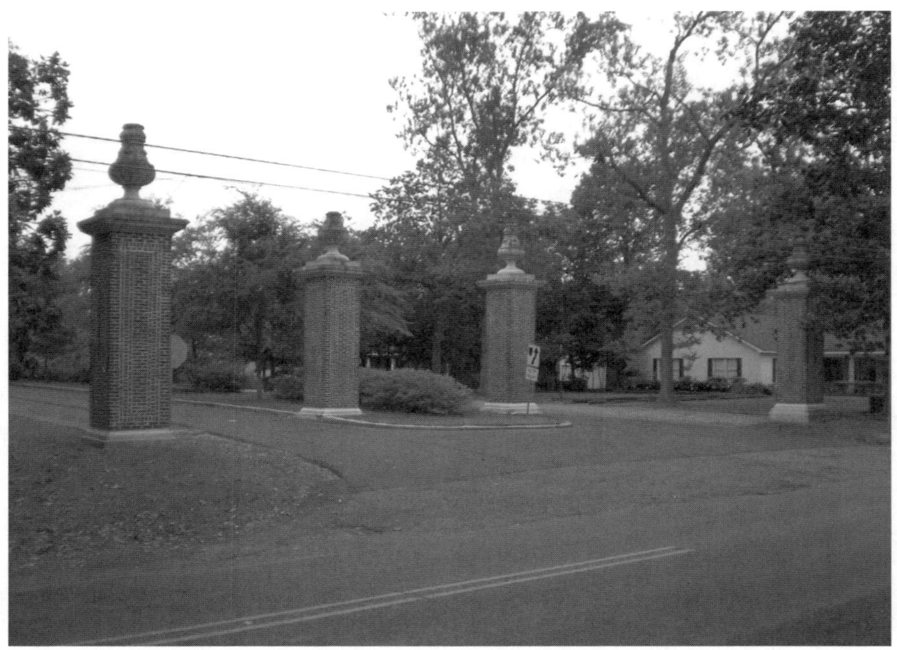

Four handmade brick and concrete ornamental pillars tower above the double boulevard entry to Steele Place. *Photo by Kenny Armstrong.*

Sanders said:

> *I used to ride here with my Uncle Tony about 1927. There was one house on Steele Boulevard, now the home of John and Lynda Thibaut. I was told that the plantation home was right at Broussard Street, during the era when Claycut was Clay Gut, gut being an engineering term for ditch. The surface was clay topped by gravel, so slippery that a car could easily slide into the ditch. We could see all the way down to Hundred Oaks. If we turned right onto what is now Acadian Thruway, the road stopped; we could look down the hill and see all the way to Perkins Road.*

The Thibaut home was built circa 1926 by the late Dr. Rufus Jackson, one of Baton Rouge's first ear, nose and throat doctors. "We love our two-story house," said Lynda Thibaut, wife of attorney John Thibaut. "It's almost Gothic style with arched doorways and windows and a curved staircase. Our driveway has a hitching post for automobiles. When cars didn't have brakes, they were tied up to posts like this."

Jayne Middleton, sharing a home with her mother on Steele Boulevard, grew up in Drehr Place and picnicked in Steele Place. Her mother, Jane, the widow of late attorney Frank Middleton, said, "I was a young bride with babies when we built in 1951. The children built forts and played on vacant lots, and a ditch ran across the property. Steele Burden laid out and landscaped my yard and taught me about gardening." (The late Burden, grandson of Captain Steele, was a landscape architect and founder of the LSU Rural Life Museum.)

In 1969, Dr. Leo and Insa Sternberg Abraham bought their Steele Boulevard lot and built a brick one-story house of four-thousand-plus square feet, designed by Town.

The boulevard is also home to David and Jeanne Curet James. "My grandparents, David and Jeanne Harvey, lived across the street when I was growing up, and this was out in the country," said Jeanne. "When David and I moved here from New Orleans, I saw seventeen houses in one day and liked this two-story wooden house built in the 1930s best. We have expanded upstairs and down, love our neighbors and our location near Calandro's grocery and St. Aloysius School."

Residents along the boulevard worked with the city and Baton Rouge Green to update the curbing and trees, present a landscape plan and install irrigation in the median.

Virginia Lobdell Jennings on Longwood Drive, author-genealogist and widow of attorney Robert Jennings, grew up on Richland Avenue. "My parents, W.A. and Virginia Young Lobdell, built on Richland in 1930, when this was a pecan grove outside the city limits and I was a freshman at Baton Rouge High," she said. "Large fields sometimes caught on fire in the fall. Daddy had big poles with huge gunny sacks on the end that he used to beat back the fire. The fire department came out when it was real bad."

John and Rosemary Campbell reside in a 1937 cypress house on Richland Avenue. "This lot was bought from Richland Corp. on June 11, 1927, by Joseph J. Gaudin and Joseph R. Clements for $1,250," said Campbell. "We moved here in 1969 and over the years have added on."

On Westmoreland Drive, off Acadian Thruway, resident Genevieve Gagliano Ricca recalled when Westmoreland was Topic. "Sam and I moved into our wood and stucco home on November 1, 1939, and when they built Acadian Thruway, it took thirty-five feet off the back of our property," she said.

Cary Saurage is renovating a brick house at the corner of Broussard and Steele. "This Town design was built by the late Marion Kahn about 1964," he said. "It has gigantic closets, and the millwork by Coco is some of the most outstanding I have ever seen anywhere."

Campbell and Robert A. "Bob" Hawthorne Jr. are principals in WARN, a nonprofit police security organization incorporated in 1989; the acronym stands for Watchful Alert Residential Neighbors.

Walnut Hills Called "Pill Hill"

"When I was a little girl, my father paid me twenty-five cents to pick up a quart of acorns; we planted them and made our own seedlings," said Yvonne Ramsey Brown, speaking of her late father, John H. Ramsey. "We had a nursery on our property on Steele Boulevard. On every lot, my father planted live oaks, many on the property line."

Like a park, Walnut Hills is a place of hills, vales and magnificent live oaks planted by the developer Ramsey in the 1940s and 1950s. The eighty acres that Ramsey and his wife, Ione Chisholm Ramsey, purchased from A.F. "Tony" Cazedessus had been a truck farm.

In horseshoe design, Walnut Hill's boundaries are Hundred Oaks Avenue, Ramsey Drive and Glenmore Avenue. Ramsey can be entered off Hundred Oaks near Acadian Thruway. Both Walnut Hills and Steele Place have Richland and Glenmore Avenues and Steele Boulevard, all of which cross Hundred Oaks Avenue. Churchill Avenue honors Great Britain's statesman Winston Churchill. Ramsey Drive was named for the developer's family, and Chatfield came from the family of his wife.

"My father intended to develop Walnut Hills right after he bought it in 1940," said Brown, the couple's only child. "When the war came along and the government froze all building materials, he farmed here and on Perkins Road in the Silverside Lane area. This was being developed while I was in preschool in 1945–46." The first filing was July 1, 1946, according to the clerk of court's office.

Ramsey built their house on a hill, with lumber coming from the old St. Joseph's Academy downtown. "Father also used this lumber to build houses across Walnut Hills," Brown said. (Update: The Ramsey house at 1955 Steele Boulevard was demolished. In 2006, owners attorney Brett Furr, his wife Renee and family moved into a new Acadian-style home, having re-salvaged and reused the materials.)

A neighbor, Dr. Henry Miller, who retired as an obstetrician-gynecologist after practicing forty-eight years, called Ramsey "a perfectionist when it came to building houses." Miller's brick and cypress home, finished in 1959, was designed by late architects Raymond Post and Benton Harelson. "The garconniere is an authentic replica of the one at Houmas House," he said. "This was the country when we moved here. So many physicians lived here that it was called 'Pill Hill.'"

Resident Delane Donahue recalled that Ramsey Drive was more like a cow path than a street, and John Ramsey on occasion had to get his tractor to pull cars out of the mud. The allure of Dawson's Creek was told by Evie Latimer, also on Ramsey Drive. "Our three children loved going to the creek. They brought home frogs, snakes, ducks and rabbits." Older resident Louise Kyle recalled picking blackberries and walking to rural mailboxes on Hundred Oaks.

Dick Hearin on Steele Boulevard said his Town-designed house of old brick was built in 1956 and purchased from Dr. Jack Jones in 1972. He likes the convenience of a "walking" neighborhood. "From my veranda I can see twenty-five oak trees," he said.

Residing on Hillside Circle in a California-style home made of St. Joseph medium brick are retired neurosurgeon Dr. Joseph Edelman and his wife, Fran. "When we built this house in 1960, it was unusual; we had so many Louisiana-style homes. Wright Adams built it and the house of Irene and the late 'Doc' Pennington on Acadian Thruway."

Blending into the landscape is the 1935 Cape Cod cypress house on Churchill Avenue, moved there in 1947 by A.M. and Eloise Heroman Hochendel. Their property on North Boulevard at Margaretta Street was taken when Acadian Thruway was constructed. "We loved this property, then considered out in the country," said Eloise. She recalled that their daughter Frances (Mrs. John Monroe) was riding the school bus home when a friend said, "Look, there goes your house!"

Jeff and Glenda Pollard, who married in 1989, live on Chatfield Avenue and used to walk in the area before they bought their brick house, once the rectory for St. James Episcopal Church built in the mid-1950s.

Walnut Hills shares police security, WARN, with Steele Place. Litter is unknown here; the acre-or-more lawns are immaculately kept.

Togetherness in Glenmore Place and Webb Park

"When Jim Thomas and Ralph Ford developed Glenmore Place in 1940, it was country, out of the city limits," said Laura Harris, who retired after teaching piano for fifty-six years. "You could feel the temperature drop when you came out here from downtown."

Since 1941, Laura and George Harris have lived in Glenmore Place, which, with Country Club Place, composes the Webb Park Neighborhood Association. With other seniors in the area, they rejoice to see hordes of young people moving into the 1940s houses. They bought their 100- by 150-foot lot for $750 and contracted with A.C. Lewis to build for $5,500. "The mortgage note was $31.04 a month plus $3 term insurance," said George. "If anything happened to me, the house would be paid off."

"Jim Thomas planted one oak tree on every lot, and if you wanted a second oak, you paid twenty-five dollars more," Laura recalled. Residents had septic tanks until about 1945, when sewage was installed. "Longwood Drive had sidewalks but we didn't. We liked the country look and wanted to cut down on traffic."

As a young wife, when George worked nights and came in at four o'clock in the morning, Laura stayed on a sleeping porch with the doors open. The house grew with the family, and a garage apartment built for their son is now used for visiting family. A plantation bell came from George's grandparents' home on Boeuf River near Monroe. "No one wants to move," said Harris. "See that big house across the street? It was a small box at first. We have seen this happen everywhere in our area."

Early resident Pansy Hebert Wright said that she and her late husband, Albert S. Wright Jr., bought their lot in 1941 and built their home, utilizing cypress, for $5,400 in 1942, paying $100 premium for the larger corner lot. Their children would take their roller skates to Longwood Drive, which had sidewalks, to skate with friends and loved to explore the woods at the end of Longwood. "Last time the electricity went out, eight neighbors checked on me," said Pansy.

One week before Pearl Harbor, December 7, 1941, Dr. Horace Tenney bought his 100- by 250-foot lot and built a ten-room brick veneer house. "There were solid woods and swamps south of us," he said. "We had to remove trees from our lot it was so thick. We had lots of blackberry bushes around us. The backyard was a wildlife habitat."

Mallory Grace said there were no streetlights when he moved into a brick veneer house on Ingleside Drive on December 15, 1941. "It cost $7,500 to build," he recalled.

The Harrises helped form the Old Town Civic Association in 1979–80, a name that gave way to the Webb Park Civic Association. Among presidents were Whit Cook, attorney, and Kent Caldwell, realtor. Now called Webb

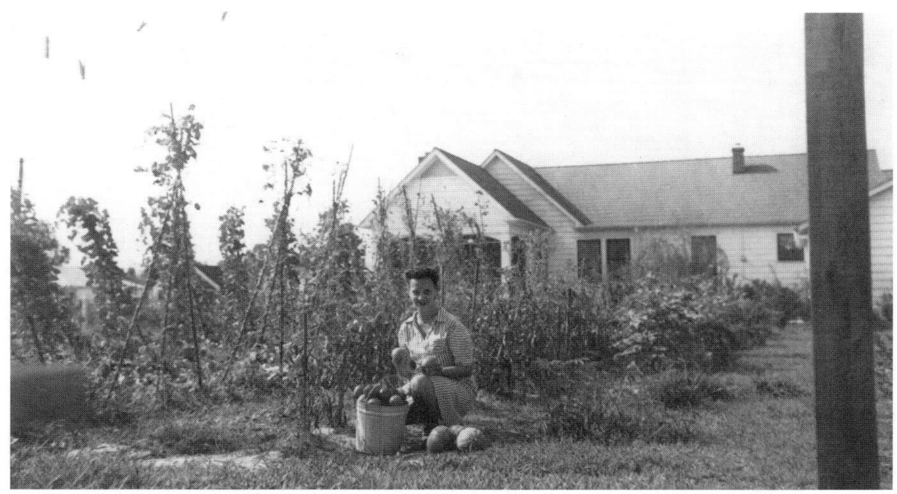

Pansy Wright gardened in her own backyard on Broussard Street at Ingleside Drive in the early 1940s. *Courtesy of Albert S. Wright III.*

Park Neighborhood Association, it is strictly a patrol watch. Some four hundred houses on eight streets are bordered by Claycut Road to the north, Glenmore to the west, Country Club to the east and Woodside to the south.

Chrystal Norwood Musgrove started Ingleside Drive's annual progressive supper. She grew up in Norwood, Louisiana, and loved her two-story house on sight because it resembled a barn. She calls it her "dream house." In 1979, her husband Larry, who had a VA loan, bought it. Extended family on Ingleside Drive includes Virginia Anders, widowed, who has lived here fifty-eight years and has two daughters, Karen Bueche and Clara Mullings, who live with their families nearby.

On Country Club Drive near the Webb Park Clubhouse and adjacent Westdale subdivision, realtor Beau Box bought a 1,500-square-foot house built in the 1940s and totally renovated it. Gutting the house, he discovered cypress floors that he had thought were plywood. A neighbor, Rucker Leake, gave him plants and helped him landscape. "The yard was hard clay (as in Clay Gut Road)," he said. "We hauled in dirt."

A neighborhood attraction is Webb Memorial Park and Golf Course, 1351 Country Club Drive. It began as Westdale Country Club in 1924, with Fannye Herzberg as the first hostess. It was a thriving social scene in the 1930s and 1940s. "Fannye was my mother-in-law, and Huey Long liked

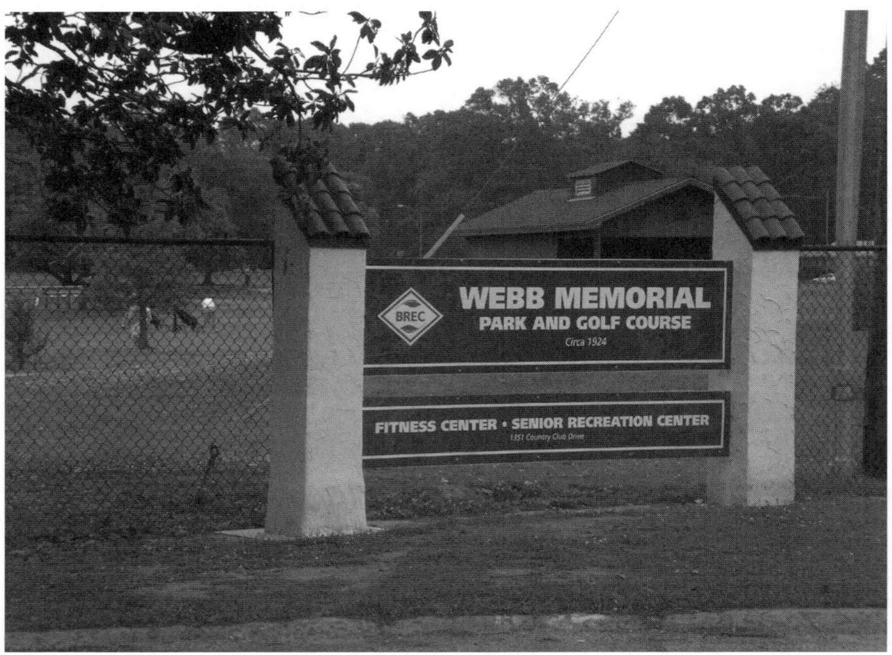

Webb Memorial Park, founded in 1924 as Westdale Country Club, honors the memory of Mayor-President Jesse Webb Jr. *Photo by Kenny Armstrong.*

her so much that he recommended her as hostess for the mansion," said Ralph Perlman, retired state budget director. "The club was sponsored by senior executives of Exxon, who needed a place for relaxation and entertainment. It began as a nine-hole golf course and expanded to eighteen holes."

Betty Moyse Simmons recalled a birthday party there once, and Frank Terrell said he went to fraternity dances and parties there in 1938–39 when the property was owned by LSU. LSU acquired the golf course and clubhouse in 1936, and on January 26, 1957, the LSU Board of Supervisors sold the land via a resolution to Baton Rouge Recreation and Park Commission (BREC). Renovations were made in 1962 under the supervision of BREC director Gene Young. After the tragic plane crash in Wisconsin in 1955 that killed thirty-one-year-old Mayor-President Jesse Webb Jr., the clubhouse was renamed Webb Memorial Park. It remains a popular place.

The Crawford Homes of Westdale

The first prefabricated construction homes in Baton Rouge, the Crawford homes, have stood the test of time in the Westdale area, where most of the houses were among this "first" in local construction. When the Crawford homes made their debut in the 1950s, they made a media splash. The lavish home of the Hamilton Crawford family at 1855 Country Club Drive was showcased in many national magazines and is still a major attraction. Designed in California, it is partially prefab construction.

The Westdale area extends from College Drive to Country Club Drive, between Hundred Oaks and Woodside Drive, and includes Westdale Terrace, Westdale Woods, Westdale Heights and some of the Webb Park vicinity leading to Country Club Place.

In 1955, Ralph Sims bought Lot One in Westdale Terrace on Woodside Drive for $27,500. He and his wife, Liza, helped select the materials for their semi-custom-built house that included old brick from Meeker Plantation

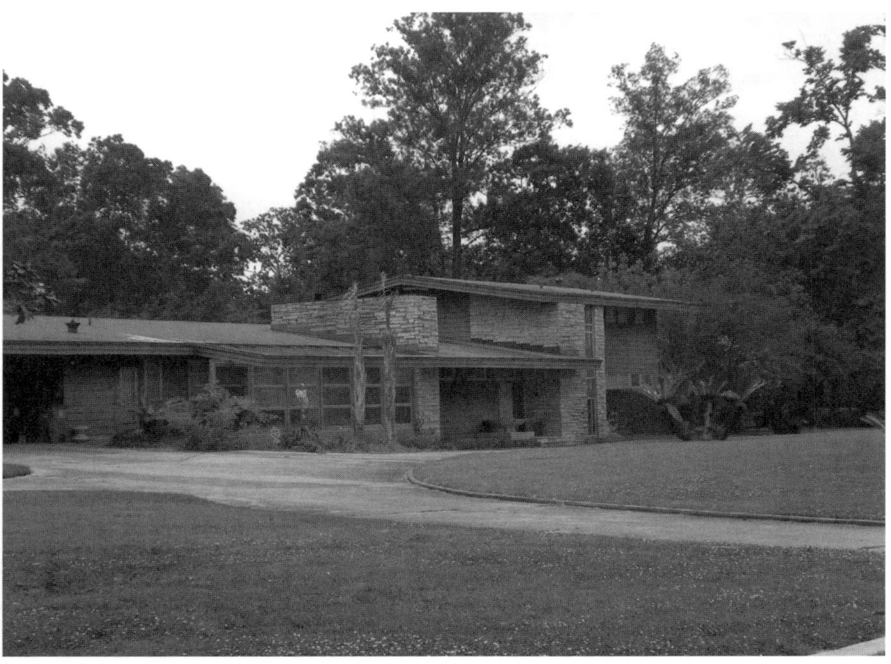

Baton Rouge's first prefabricated houses were built by Hamilton Crawford. The Crawford family home, 1855 Country Club Drive, was partially prefabricated. *Photo by Kenny Armstrong.*

near Bunkie. A retired banker and prominent citizen, Ralph said that he and Liza liked their 1,600-square-foot house with a courtyard-garden area, and they reared three daughters there.

Sims had worked with Hamilton Crawford from 1953 to 1965, when Crawford built Crofton, Maryland, he said. "Mr. Crawford had high standards, used good architects and materials. He had sidewalks, curbs, gutters and streetlights installed."

Tommy Bartkiewicz is renovating and enlarging his family house on Abelia Drive, once the home of his parents. His boyhood memories include watching the tractors at Westdale Elementary School when it was being built in 1958, riding bikes downtown and catching the ferry across the Mississippi River. He and his wife, Jackie, remember when the only buildings on College Drive were the school and WAIL radio station, housed in a World War II Quonset hut.

Walking her dogs along the bike trail directly behind the Crawford home, teacher Bonnie Baker said she grew up with her family on Silliman Avenue. She recalled happy times with her siblings playing ball with the dogs. "The balls would fly over the fence of the Crawford house. We would have to walk all around to the front door. It was like going to 'God's House' to us. We would knock and ask if we could go inside the yard and retrieve our balls, and they were always very nice to us." She also recalled playing in the streets and staying out late on Friday evenings, a carefree time when parents had no worries about safety and were close to other families.

A Hidden Nook in the Center of the City: Glenwood

The names Bardwell and Holloway go together, and longtime residents of Glenwood subdivision still say the names like the team they were. Starting in 1955, Robert Ashton "Bob" Holloway and Stanford O. "Stan" Bardwell developed Glenwood, off College Drive near the Westdale Golf Course.

"Dad started building after World War II when veterans returned but could not find affordable houses," said Stan Bardwell Jr. "Dad owned Bardwell and Sons. He and Mr. Holloway loved to help those who needed an affordable place to live. In North Baton Rouge, they built houses in Delmont Village, Victory Place, on both sides of Plank Road and in the Redemptorist area. When families started making $200 a month and could find no place to live, they proposed small houses with built-in ranges on curb-and-gutter streets, for payments of $50 to $55 a month.

"They then spread out to the center of town with houses in College Drive Heights, on Bardwell and Holloway Streets and in the Westdale and College Drive area."

Secluded and heavily treed, Glenwood has only one exit street, Berkshire Avenue, that leads to College Drive near the circle entrance to Jefferson Highway. "If you throw a dart at a city map and go for the center portion of the city limits, you will hit Glenwood," said Alden S. Holloway, who resides with his family in Glenwood.

The civic association's first president in 1974 was Stan Bardwell Jr., who purchased his lot as an investment. "Dad and Bob Holloway each kept three lots as their profit in the deal," said Bardwell. "I bought one in 1965, the year I finished LSU Law School. I borrowed money from Louisiana National Bank and paid $100 a month for four or five years."

He and his wife, Leslie, reared their three children there in a brick house with a front porch and lushly planted lot adjacent to the property of Phil Witter, the former Cedar Grove Plantation.

Alden Holloway grew up in Glenwood. "In 1957, my parents built their dream house on two lots. Three days before I turned six years old, we moved in." Married to Beth Ferguson, Alden, an architect and contractor, said they enjoy their 5,500-square-foot house with a large pool and decks. "It's a heck of a party house."

Alden and Stan share memories of their fathers, who encouraged one another, and of the "Talking House" in College Drive Heights, off College between Westdale and Valley Park. "It was the talk of the town," said Bardwell, "a builder's showcase home with the latest equipment and gadgetry. When people went on a tour, the furniture 'spoke.' Little microphones had been planted in the furniture."

Jim and Zelda Harvey purchased the "Talking House," and their daughter Janice Harvey Pellar remembered it well. "My parents bought the house in 1954 when I was about three years old," she said. "College Drive was paved only to our two streets, Bardwell and Holloway, then became a dirt road going down the hill toward Perkins Road. College Drive stopped at Bienville Towers. On College by Corporate Boulevard, there were horse stables."

Taking Goodwood Boulevard Out Jefferson Highway

The Glamour of Goodwood

The romantic history of Goodwood Place goes back to Goodwood Plantation days in the nineteenth century when thoroughbred horses raced a one-mile track from Lobdell Avenue, now Independence Park, to the entrance at Jefferson Highway and Goodwood Avenue. Race results were sent out by carrier pigeon.

Dr. Samuel G. Laycock, a young physician in the early 1850s, built the Greek Revival plantation home on Goodwood Avenue on twenty acres, the remainder of a four-thousand-acre land grant from England's King George III to Thomas Hutchings. From England, he named it Goodwood, near Sussex. A racecourse still exists at the English Goodwood.

"This was an era of grandeur and glamour," said Kevin Babb, president of the Goodwood Property Owners Association. "We are thrilled with our Goodwood history."

The plantation was once the center of a thriving sugar cane industry; Laycock added the farming of two thousand acres of sugar cane to his medical practice.

Goodwood Plantation Home was one of the first houses in the area to have running water, supplied by large attic cisterns. The mansion is reached by a gravel driveway that loops to form a semicircle in front of the home's veranda. It has a neoclassical façade and a broad second-story

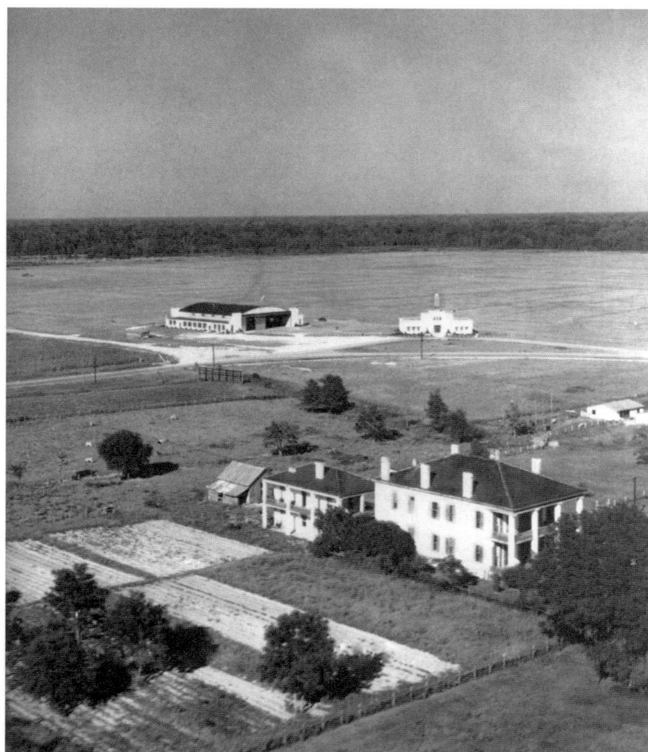

This 1929 aerial shows Goodwood Plantation Home and servants' quarters and the Downtown Baton Rouge Airport, now Independence Park. *Courtesy of Jack Whitaker.*

gallery supported by four round columns, and it was shown on an open-door tour in 1964. The built-in washstands with marble tops and hand-painted Wedgwood china washbowls were a revelation to visitors.

Through the years, when the family of Louis Winbourne Babin and his wife, Belle Stanard Babin, lived there, it was the setting for elaborate teas, parties and a Hollywood movie production by Otto Preminger, *Hurry Sundown*. At one time it was a plush nightclub called the Grove. Today, it is the private residence of Tom Babin, one of four children of the late L.W. and Belle Babin.

"When I lived there several weeks in 1951, there were slot machines still there," said Mary Pearl Stanard Lorio, niece of the late L.W. Babin and the first Miss Baton Rouge in 1948. She also attended LSU with actress and friend Joanne Woodward but left after one year to marry Clarence Lorio.

She and her cousin, Sally Ratelle Brown, remember when *Hurry Sundown* was filmed in 1966. "I met Michael Caine, Jane Fonda and Otto Preminger," said Lorio. "Otto loved Aunt Belle, who had been the first Belle of Baton Rouge."

Brown was impressed by the servants' quarters. "Each section had a large room downstairs with a massive fireplace and an upstairs bedroom," she recalled. "The upstairs could only be reached by exterior stairs. I loved playing back there because it was spooky, and Aunt Belle would tell us there was a ghost in the garconniere, probably her way to keep us out of there." The garconniere is all that remains, she said.

Lorio and Brown said their late uncle, a brilliant Harvard graduate, was very eccentric. "He and Aunt Belle had four children and lots of property," Brown stated. "Tom Drive was named for Tom, who lives in the 'big house.' Albert, another son, lives on Goodwood near Jefferson Highway. Annabelle Street in Goodwood Place was named for the Babins' late daughter. They also have a son, Louis Augustus 'Gus.'"

When Goodwood Place was established in the late 1930s and 1940s, a promotional booklet detailing the development was published by the late C.J. Brown, L.W. Babin and John T. Laycock. "I'm pretty sure my father wrote it," said C.J. "Cy" Brown Jr. "He was an educator known statewide before he became a realtor." In extravagant prose and beautiful illustrations, the booklet tells the story of 350 acres of choice land, with trees of every description and spacious graveled streets carved from the historic plantation.

Boundaries are Jefferson Highway to the south, Florida Boulevard to the north, Cloud Drive and Fairfax to the west and East Airport Drive to the east. "Our association also includes Carter Avenue and a section of Old Hammond Highway," said Babb. "We have small neighborhoods within our whole area. We send out 1,400 newsletters for the 1,400 homeowners, have annual dues, parties and a phone tree that deters crime by alerting households in emergencies."

American Park Builders of Chicago helped develop a nature park place, originally planning a lake, where Goodwood Park is located. Five acres were dedicated for a school site and playgrounds, and commercial buildings could not be constructed without approval of 80 percent of property owners within a radius of six hundred feet from the site. Also, a 1990 parish-wide soil survey showed that Goodwood's soil has characteristics of the soil in the Felicianas, with a deposit that occurred during the ice age when the glaciers moved here. The site is shown to be one of the most elevated sections in the city, with elevation of fifty-two feet.

Development of individual houses continued through the 1940s. Dr. Chet Coles's house on Goodwood Avenue, built in 1936, was called "the Coca-Cola House" because the late Tom Daigre of Baton Rouge Coca-Cola Company built it.

Kevin and Carol Babb said that Seven Oaks Avenue was originally planned as a major street extending from the park, to be called St. Charles Avenue. "We paid $67,000 in 1986 for our home, and the property value has greatly increased," he said. Rather than move, when their family increased, they added on.

Ed and Nell Fetzer bought a house on LaSalle for $14,500 in the 1950s, improved it and sold it for over $300,000. They built their six-thousand-square-foot house on Seven Oaks Avenue across from Goodwood Park in 1969 and, a year later, built Goodwood Village, a small mall fronting Jefferson Highway, where Nell has Fetzer's Interiors. Nell designed the Mediterranean-style house and a two-story guesthouse and studio used by Ed, a painter. They reared four children there. They like the country atmosphere and five-minute proximity to grocery, restaurant or church.

Louise "Weesie" Prosser said that all ages merge in Goodwood Place. When she and Dr. Charles Prosser moved into their house forty-four years ago, they had five girls and one boy. They later had two more children. "Most houses were here already," she said. "There were no curbs, gutters, sidewalks, and there was a small two-lane road. We had ditches and no storm sewer." She recalled when citizens saved Goodwood Park. "BREC thought not enough people were using it then, so we went to the zoning commission and council meetings and fought for the park. Now it is filled with young people. BREC built tennis courts and improved it."

The aura of the past stays here, where lots are large and restrictions are strict. Many stately houses grace the area.

Going Home to Tara

The drive along Tara Boulevard and on the side streets is a scenic delight following the theme of *Gone with the Wind*. The cruise down Oakley, Tallyho, Trinity, Wakefield, Cottage, Longview, Beechgrove, Ashland and others brings to mind great plantations, of which many remain tourist attractions.

"We got together and chose the names," attorney Rolfe McCollister, one of the developers, recalled. "We bought 315 acres from Dr. Howard Witter." Other developers were George McNutt and James Lieux, along with Clifford Ourso, Dr. Carl Baldridge, Wally Wells, George Caldwell and Witter.

Developers donated land for Tara Club, built an Olympic-size swimming pool to attract residents and gave land for tennis courts as well, said McCollister.

Tara High School opened in August 1970, at the outset of the development, and is part of the community.

At each end of Tara Boulevard that extends from Goodwood Boulevard to Old Hammond Highway, the seasonal flowerbed and scrolled wooden Tara sign bid a welcome into the neighborhood of 620 homes. The subdivision is also bordered by Chevelle Drive and by Crescent Drive, which backs up to Ward's Creek. Its spacious look emanates from large lots and a required sixty-foot setback line for boulevard homes.

The Tara Civic Association, founded by Mike McDonald, has remained strong and community minded. For more than thirty years, Dr. Joseph P. "Doc" Roumain has served as treasurer on a twelve-member board. The association has a director, newsletter, Christmas lighting contest and patrols by off-duty police officers.

"In the last three years we have accomplished a lot," said Margaret Landry, president, often seen working in flowerbeds on the boulevard. Naming projects, she concluded with, "We kept Baton Rouge Community College from being held temporarily at Tara High School, which would have greatly increased the traffic from 4:00 to 10:00 p.m."

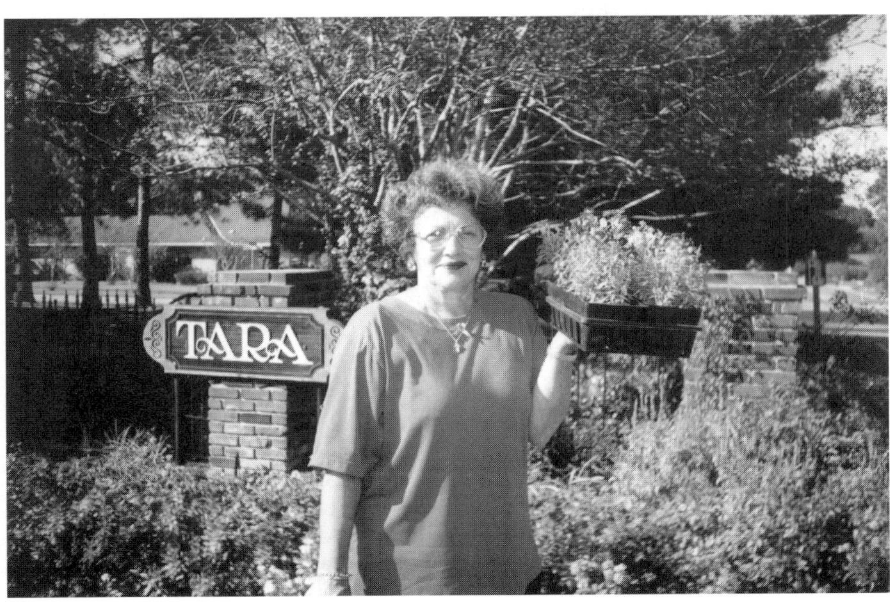

Margaret Landry works the flowerbeds at Tara Boulevard and Old Hammond Highway. She and her husband, Windom, are longtime residents and volunteers.

"Everyone works as a team," said Landry, who moved to the subdivision in 1979 after marrying Windom "Win" Landry, who built his 3,700-square-foot Crescent Drive home in 1972. Both are retired from Bell South. Margaret writes *Tara Talk*, the newsletter; Win types, edits and formats it on the computer. He just computerized the association's financial statement and budget.

They praise the committees, which include a welcoming committee for new families. "Our number one focus is security," they said, "and Dale Ulkins, security chairman, gives his all to this untiring work."

On the boulevard, "Doc" and Natalie Roumain had their home built by Durward Gully in 1967 when their children were in high school. They selected the plans for their home of 2,200 square feet on a 110- by 150-foot lot and enjoy entertaining and family gatherings. Since 1949, Roumain has been in business as an optometrist. They are community activists.

Mike and Bobbie Nesbit McDonald moved to Trudeau Drive to be close to the new Tara High School in 1969 after living in Melrose. Their three children finished Tara High School and have college degrees. A chemical engineer who retired from Exxon in 1995, Mike remains active in the association.

Dale and Kathy Ulkins (the former Kathy Kovacs) are Hungarians from Coudersport, Pennsylvania. They have lived in Baton Rouge all twenty-five years of their marriage, and they have a son and daughter. All four—along with Hilda Edward, septuagenarian on the Tara board since its inception—decorated the entrances of Tara Boulevard for every holiday. Dale Ulkins also plays guitar for children's groups and composes songs for children. He is listed in the directory of Louisiana musicians for the State Library and performs for clubs and at libraries.

Richard Landry said that his wife, Carolyn Abadie Landry, is living her dream, as she has always wanted to live in Tara. They reside near her parents, Leo and Lois Abadie, on Ashland Drive, where Carolyn, youngest of five children, was reared. Twice they won best children's decorations in the Christmas lighting contest. "We both worked at Disney World in Orlando during the summer when we attended LSU," said Carolyn. Richard did research for the new Tara directory, and they are active at Our Lady of Mercy Catholic Church. The active couple enjoys entertaining.

One Man's Dream: Jefferson Place

"Puna would be so thrilled to see what has happened here," said Metro Councilwoman Mary Frey Eaton, speaking of her late husband, L.W. "Puna" Eaton Jr., the developer of Jefferson Place.

Returning to Baton Rouge in 1952 with a family of four, who had lived in California while he served in Korea, Eaton wanted to establish a nice place for families to rear their children. He found the 160-acre Pope tract in the middle of Witter property; the Witters agreed to sell him enough property for a single boulevard and lots on one side. The Eaton house, the first one built, is located on the left side of McCarroll Boulevard, the single entrance off Jefferson Highway.

Eaton sold every one of the one-hundred- by two-hundred-foot lots at thirty-five dollars a front foot. He did not want spec houses or lookalikes. His family lot, two hundred square feet, was chosen because it was uneven. Wright Adams built more than fifty houses in Jefferson Place.

Mary Frey Eaton selected proper names for the streets, called drives. McCarroll was her paternal grandmother's maiden name, and Boyce was named for Jane and the late Jimmy Boyce, who reared their family in a white brick home at the corner of McCarroll and Boyce. Others were named for friends, including Conway for Bob and Joyce Conway and Richards for the late Bill Richards and Julia Richards Hamilton.

Bob and Joyce Conway live in a two-story home built by their son, Grant Conway, on a cul-de-sac extension of Richards Drive, opened up in recent years after construction of apartment complexes on Jefferson Highway. Before that, they lived for thirty-five years on Murphy and fourteen months on Conway. "Joyce and I have known one another since grammar school," said Bob. He finished Catholic High and she finished St. Joseph Academy, when both were located downtown.

On a hill across the street, Walter and Diane Kirtland live in a two-story, six-thousand-square-foot stucco Italian-style home. In the 1950s, Mary Belle Huff Kirtland, Walter's mother, bought the property from the Witter family.

The Witter land was once called Cedar Lodge, a plantation that abutted Windrush, the Burden plantation. "The best quail and dove hunting used to be in the middle of where Bocage is today," said businessman-horseman Phil Witter on Jefferson Highway. "There was a big lake right there. Cedar Lodge was a Spanish land grant of 1,800 acres, and I can remember as a kid riding my horse all the way back to the Burden landing strip." He said the property came from his mother's family, descending from William Garig to her father, William Phillips Connell. Phil and Sandi Witter's home and their Live Oaks Arabian Stables are located on what was once the plantation. The Kirtlands sold some of their property to Amov Construction in 1984 to develop Jefferson Place Apartments and Jefferson Place Office Park.

Mary Frey Eaton Stewart was twenty-four years old and had just married Dexter Stewart when her father died. She is active in the association, which also includes Bocage subdivision, accessible through McCarroll Drive, developed by Tom Singletary.

"Our father bought the Witter property in the 1950s as the family needed a larger house," said Dorsey Singletary Peek. Six children (three girls, three boys) grew up on Bocage Boulevard in an English Tudor home, now the home of Alex and C.C. Lewis. They recalled happy years of riding horses and of having friends stay overnight with their large family.

Among early homes built were those of Chuck and Ruth McCoy on Bocage Boulevard, now the home of Sarah and Dr. E.D. Bateman Jr., and Dr. and Mrs. Milton Harris, also on the boulevard. Since 1986, Penny and Henry

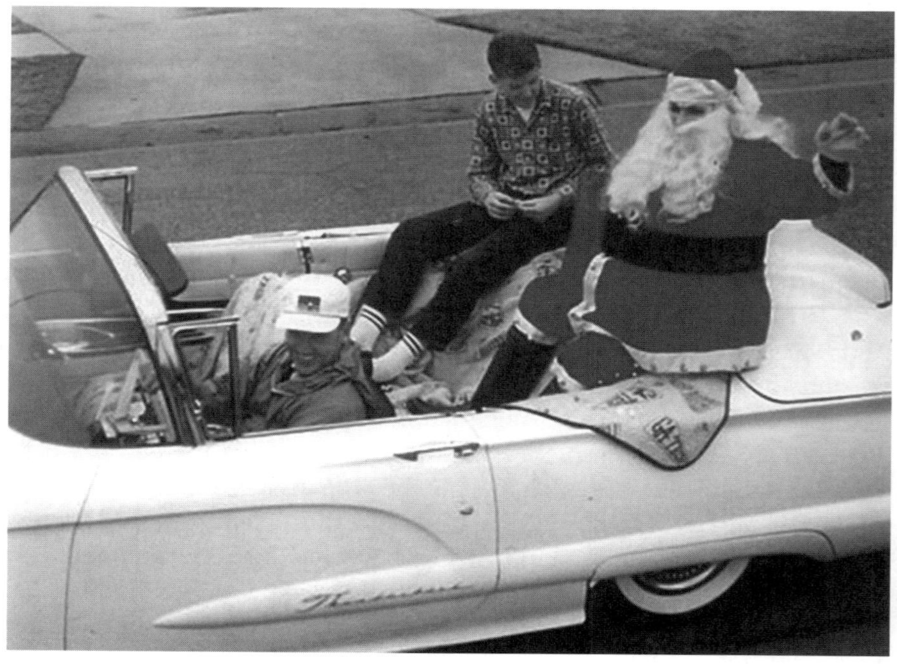

Lewis "Puna" Eaton and Floyd "Flop" Womack (Santa) started Jefferson Place subdivision's Christmas parade. Greg Eaton is shown at center, 1959. *Courtesy of Mary Frey Eaton.*

"Chick" Miller have lived in Bocage Estates, a Phil Witter development. Dorsey and Mac Peek live on Torrance Drive.

Since 1954, the strong civic association, which covers Jefferson Place and Bocage, has sponsored a Christmas Eve Parade, started by Puna Eaton with "Flop" Womack as Santa Claus. Activities include a welcoming committee that takes a cake or loaf of bread to newcomers. Members of the welcoming committee are never surprised to find that newcomers are old friends who have grown up and returned to reside here.

Westminster and Pine Park Pairing

"When we bought three hundred acres and helped develop Westminster in 1955, it was the first subdivision out of town," recalled Thomas R. Pruyn, who was president of the Westminster Development Corp. at the time. "We had to get city water run out there."

Pruyn worked in real estate with his father, Clarence Pruyn Sr., and his brother, Clarence Pruyn Jr., when the subdivision was built. After the first three filings opened, the Pruyns built the first fifty-plus houses. Lots were sold, and other builders participated.

Early residents remember the absence of fire protection and streetlights and the lack of places to shop. The opposite is true today. Residents praise the neighborhood's accessibility to Interstates 10 and 12, Airline Highway and shopping centers and cite the low crime rate and the St. George Fire Station on Jefferson Highway.

Westminster is linked with Pine Park. The adjacent subdivisions open to Jefferson Highway and are enclosed in what past civic association president Tommy Loyacono called a "locked-in area." Borders are Jefferson Highway to Norfolk Drive and Drusilla Drive to Pine Park Drive. One civic association governs both, with some six hundred households.

"We're Westminster Pine Park Proud," said John Pray, association president, who designed logos and entrance signs to the subdivision and organized decorating contests, the local garden club and the Christmas luminaries.

Richard Rolston, PhD, has lived on Drusilla Drive since 1963. His father, W.A. Rolston Sr., was a silent partner in the development. "My father's parents were from England," said Rolston. "I sat down with them, we got out a map of London and looked up major streets, like Downing, Chelsea and Fleet, and wrote the names on the plat. Westminster came from Westminster Abbey." He and his wife, Sally, said they like their neighborhood and the elementary school—where Sally volunteers—their private, acre-and-a-half-yard and beautiful trees. His father was a contractor. "When we built our house, it was the last lot at the end of Drusilla, and beyond us was a gravel road. Now all that has built up."

Pine Park opened in the mid-1960s. Its developer was the late James Hamilton Smith, whose son Jim "Jimbo" Smith and family live in Pine Park. "I was about sixteen years old when dad opened Pine Park," he said. "He got trees from the state forestry department and planted pines everywhere. Now some are sixty to seventy feet tall."

"Pine Park had not been developed when we first lived in Westminster," said Bill Elam, who has worked closely with Pray since the association was re-formed in 1994. "Like many associations, it would be strong then dormant and reactivate when needed. In 1978, Wards Creek's erosion problems brought the association to life. The late Councilman Mike Roubique helped us get concrete lining for Ward's Creek. Recently, with the help of Fred Raiford, Department of Public Works, the area saw the installation of flapper valves on the storm drains."

Pine Park includes Pine Park, Pine Ridge, Pine Crest Streets and a portion of other streets located toward the southeast, including Fleet Drive.

Ten residents who formed a corporation to generate funds founded Westminster Swimming Pool in 1969. Shares of stock were sold, and each stockholder pays annual dues. The two well-lighted tennis courts at the club have been resurfaced.

The association has a monthly newsletter and security patrol, sponsors social events and has published a cookbook of residents' favorite family recipes.

THE WORLD OF INNIS: THE HILL

Those entering the Hill through handsome brick walls on either side of North Bluebonnet Road, off Jefferson Highway, enter a slice of history. Before it became Inniswold Farm in the early 1900s, it was Burden property. Here are twenty-eight acres, once the northwest corner of the farm, developed in the early 1960s by General Charles Duchein and John McCain. Today, the Hill has approximately fifty homes and seventeen town houses.

To many, the Hill is synonymous with the McInnis family, many of whom grew up on the land as descendants of Douglas Emmitt (D.E.) and Ella Oliphant McInnis. A grandson, Weldon McInnis, said, "Paw Paw was a sawmill man from Hattiesburg, Mississippi, who came to Baton Rouge in 1919, after buying 1,500 acres from a member of the Burden family." Weldon and others in the family grew up in the area called "the Hill."

Inniswold is a Scottish word that means "the world of Innis." Weldon stated, "Inniswold Farm encompassed land in a southerly point adjoining the then George Pollack property (subsequently Jimmy Swaggart ministries) with a westward line of Bluebonnet in a northerly line to I-12 and eastward to the Istrouma Baptist Church, and southerly along Cedarcrest and Pine Park on the east, back to Jefferson Highway."

The McInnis "Big House," where the grandparents lived, later became a favorite teen recreational center, the Acadian Club, much of which burned down. Marking the approximate site is McInnis Road, a narrow road still in place.

"Our grandfather converted Burden's sugar cane plantation to conventional farming, primarily cotton and corn," said Dr. A.K. McInnis, retired surgeon, another grandson. "He bought the land from John Burden. [John was a cousin of the late Steele Burden.] Our grandfather also built homes for six of his nine children on the 'hill side' of Jefferson Highway."

"These are Paw Paw's journals," said Weldon, opening a thick thirteen-by fifteen-inch tome with "Inniswold" imprinted at the top of each page.

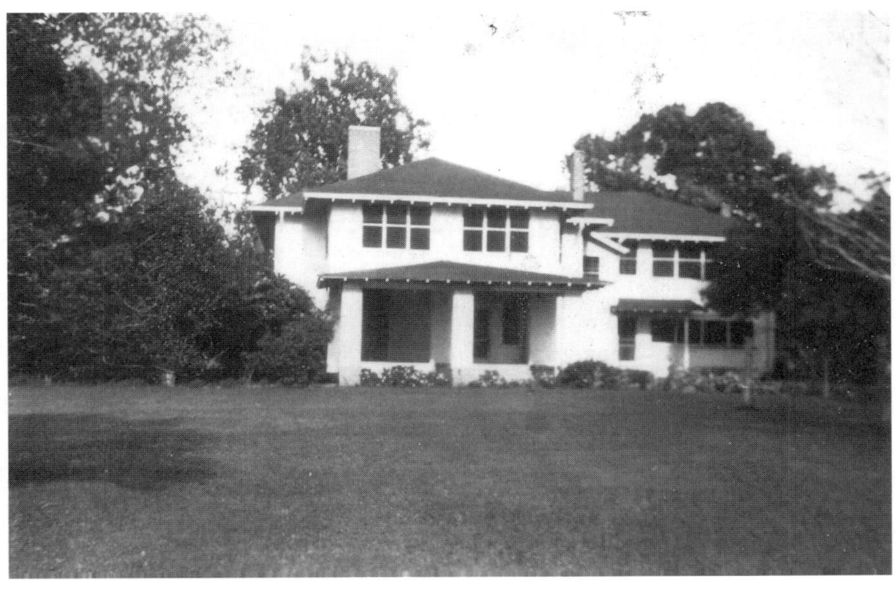

"The Big House" of Inniswold Farm stood on present-day Jefferson Highway near Bluebonnet Boulevard, 1930. *Courtesy of D.E. "Skipper" McInnis IV.*

D.E. McInnis carefully recorded wages of workers by name and job (bean, corn or cotton picker, wood hauler, etc.), told conditions of the crops and added personal notes. A going pay rate was one dollar per day. On January 26, 1929, he wrote: "Very bad farming weather. More rain this month than any January since I lived in Louisiana." March 23, 1929: "Never saw corn and beans come up so soon as this year. Up in six days." In April 1933 he recorded a hailstorm, crops ruined and windows knocked out. "Ungodly weather for farming," then, "My God, why so much rain for no use?" Happy notes: "March 2, 1929 was our most beautiful anniversary. Very happy we were."

Today, first cousins Weldon, A.K. and Charles McInnis and Frances M. Fish, among the grandchildren of McInnis, reside with their respective families in nearby Jefferson Place.

To develop the Hill, Duchein and McCain purchased and put together three tracts of land. Lots average 110 by 150 feet. More than 40 percent of the residences were built by James Sumrow in partnership with Edward "Red" Reynolds, realtor. The Reynoldses live in a town house here and the Sumrows in Jamestown Court, which Sumrow developed in the early 1970s. "The town houses in the Hill were the first built in Baton Rouge," said Sumrow.

The one entrance/exit allows the children to ride their bikes and roller skate in a protected environment. North Bluebonnet Road curves into Hilltrace Avenue, where the town houses stand. Other thoroughfares are Winddrift and Blueridge Avenues and Ridgetop Drive.

"Charlie Duchein and John McCain built this first town house unit, where I live, in 1974," said Betty Phelps. She and her late husband, C. Paul Phelps, bought the town house on Hilltrace Avenue, purchased a small adjacent lot, installed a pool and extended the town house to 3,800 square feet. Formerly occupied by the Ducheins, it displays the marine corps insignia in sandstone on the entry porch wall. Wooden beams from an old New Orleans warehouse and 18-foot ceilings, family antiques and chandeliers, along with an enclosed patio, add to the charm.

Resident since 1977, Anne Burford Williams said that she and her husband, Paul, were looking for a smaller home as their children got older. Both she and Williams were widowed, with children, when they married in 1970. "This house had already been built. We refurbished it and enlarged the patio," she said.

Attorney Jim McIlwain, his wife Terri and their three children moved into their brick home built in 1968 in 1997. They renovated the house and updated the sunroom. "We have good participation in the association," he said. "We keep an eye out on our traffic light on Jefferson at the entrance and on what is going on around us and watch development in our area, as this affects us." The Hill Property Owners Association has a board of directors and annual voluntary dues, sponsors spring and Christmas parties and oversees maintenance of lighting at the entry walls and landscaping.

A second-generation Hill resident, Richard A. Gwin on North Bluebonnet, served as president of the Hill Property Owners Association from 1992 to 1994; his late father, Fred Gwin, was its first president in the early 1970s. "Our homeowners were assessed $500 a home for the Norwegian brick walls at the entry," he said. "We maintan the underground sprinklers, landscaping and lighting."

Longtime residents include Bob Davidge, retired administrator, Our Lady of the Lake Regional Medical Center, and retired physician Dr. Mortimer Currier.

Inniswold and Jefferson Terrace Once Vast Farmland

Like the Hill, the much-larger Inniswold and Jefferson Terrace Subdivisions were part of the vast farmland of D.E. and Ella Oliphant McInnis. Their umbrella civic association takes in 1,100 households and a number of pocket subdivisions. "My grandfather bought about 1,500 acres one afternoon on a handshake with John C. Burden," said Dr. A.K. McInnis Jr., a retired surgeon.

> *Grandfather was in the brokerage business, one of the first here. When his comptroller stole $250,000 from him in 1931–32 and went to Angola, my father took over and paid off the debt rather than declare bankruptcy. When I was fifteen, my family started selling off the land to repay the debtors, and the first sale took place about 1938 or 1939.*
>
> *The first subdivision developed was located near a cornfield across from our grandparents' home, which we called the Big House. The late O.M. Pollard helped form a business syndicate with him. Dr. Claude McConnell, a retired family physician, was in that first group of about twelve partners that included other physicians.*

McInnis recalled boyhood days. Before boarding the school bus, he would shoot his limit of doves, and when he returned home, he would get on his

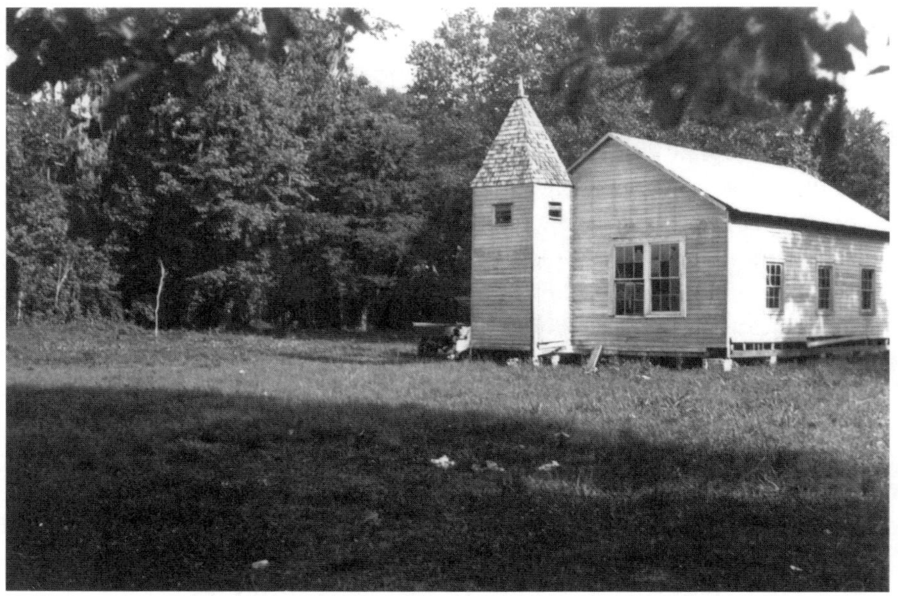

This small steepled church once stood on McInnis Farm, home now of Inniswold and other subdivisions. *Courtesy of D.E. "Skipper" McInnis IV.*

horse and shoot his limit of quail. "It was a sportsman's paradise out here." He also recalled that Jefferson Highway was a gravel road, a popular route to Gonzales for those wanting to take the River Road to New Orleans.

Residents who built homes right after World War II when Jefferson Highway was a two-lane thoroughfare find today's growth phenomenal.

Art Lamm, retired educator, said that Durward Gully and Howard Poor developed most of both subdivisions, with Inniswold first. Lamm served as president of the Inniswold–Jefferson Terrace Civic Association.

Inniswold is bordered by Jefferson Highway, Westminster, I-10 and Floynell Drive, with more than 375 households. Jefferson Terrace came later, bordered by Floynell Drive south to Airline and Jefferson Highways, and has 725 households. Lamm recalled the big move to develop Jefferson Terrace after Jefferson Terrace Elementary School opened in 1958.

Lamm said that Durward Gully donated a large rectangular plot of land for a middle school that was never built. It is bordered by Azroc Avenue, Upton Drive, Dwyerwood Avenue and Lorange Drive near the large Blue Cross building.

The beautiful BREC Park on Cal Road was built on land donated by Gully, who also built a swimming pool. The popular facility has stock and memberships. The neighborhood assisted the club in building a new shelter near the open pool.

Former resident Barbara Gully of Raleigh, North Carolina, lived in five houses in Jefferson Terrace when she was growing up. "I loved it," she said. "Early on, friends thought they had to pack a lunch to visit us it was so remote. Bocage was then Twin Cedars; the only thing there was a wooden grocery store called Twin Cedars."

Some streets were named for family.

> *My father's middle name was Houston, and Gail was named for my younger sister, the late Gail Gully Poirier. Baton Rouge already had a Barbara Street. Floynell Drive was named after Floy Poor, Howard's wife, and Nell for Durward's wife. When Daddy bought the land, Cal, Oliphant, Inniswold and Bluebonnet Roads were like a triangle with huge tracts and old houses. He developed all around that square. Then when he and Howard Poor split the partnership, Daddy owned it and kept developing.*

Barbara said that he died in 1994 and owned all the way from Gail Drive to where the Mall of Louisiana is today. Her former husband, Ken Owens, developed most of Ridgely Drive.

Memories told by longtime residents include that of James Crane on Cal Road, called Route 1 when he and his wife moved there in 1952 before Jefferson Terrace was developed.

> *We bought an acre and had our house built. We had rows and rows in our backyard. It appeared to have been peas planted all the way to Oliphant Road. We called it 'our old pea patch.' Inniswold was a great place to rear the children, with room for their dogs. We had pine trees and owls. Then, when Tealwood and Cottage Hills were developed, it destroyed our habitat for the owls.*

In 1993, Billy Gibson, journalist, predicted the growth of the area. Among those interviewed were Marcell and Harold Richard on Bluebonnet, the first family to settle on the open pastureland owned by the McInnis family. They bought five acres for $3,000 at 2.5 percent interest. Marcell remembered open fields and grain silos dominating the terrain and groceries being delivered to the door.

Elizabeth Price, who has lived for fifty years on Bluebonnet Road, moved in with her late husband, Robert, on three and a half acres in 1948. "We actually built our two-bedroom house and had one child when we moved in, then had our second in January. Richard did not believe in going into debt, and we built as we got the materials and money. We ended up having three bedrooms, two baths, dining and living rooms and a den."

Across the two subdivisions, interviewees eagerly awaited construction of Bluebonnet Parkway by the Department of Public Works. The Parkway was planned to relieve heavy traffic on Bluebonnet Road, with the new Parkway to access from Gail, Oliphant and Cal.

The area was praised for its family atmosphere, neighborhood pool, BREC park and convenient location. East Baton Rouge sheriff's deputies who live or work in the area voluntarily patrol. "We have fun out here," said Lamm.

Traveling Out Perkins Road

The Lakes and University Gardens

"Even when the economy slumped in the mid-1980s, our area remained stable," said Paul Naquin Jr., who grew up in the home on Morning Glory Avenue where he and his wife, Ann, now live. His childhood memories capture boating, fishing and camping overnight on an island (no longer there) in University Lake.

Here, million-dollar-plus mansions, such as preservationist-businessman Bob Dean's home at the juncture of East Lakeshore Drive and Stanford Avenue, contrast with small, historic homes along cozy, tree-lined streets.

Octogenarian Verdie Reece Perkins, the real estate agent for Henry W. Jolly in the early 1930s when the property was sold and developed, has a 1936 plat of University Gardens. Several hundred lots are bounded by Perkins Road to East Lakeshore Drive and from Stanford to Hollydale Avenues. The "dale streets" included are Hollydale, Ferndale, Cedardale, Glendale, Myrtledale and Cherrydale Avenues. Cross streets are Morning Glory and several blocks of Marigold and Hyacinth.

"This was all Jolly property," said Perkins, showing where he wrote $2,000 on a lakefront lot sold in the 1930s. Recent lots sold went for $450,000.

The grandson of developer Henry W. Jolly, Henry William "Bill" Jolly III described an idyllic childhood in Stanford Place, then his grandfather's

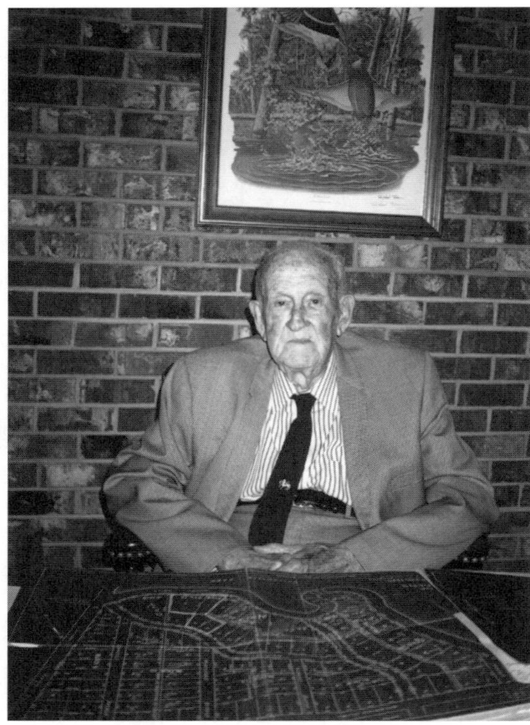

Verdie Reece Perkins, prominent realtor, shown looking over the 1936 plat of University Gardens, which he developed.

pasture, for a *Journal* article on Stanford Place in May 2000. The son of Dr. and Mrs. Henry W. Jolly Jr. said,

> *Grandfather married Etta Blouin, who inherited a large amount of property that included University Gardens. An 1848 plantation map includes a 2,000-acre tract, which was the Etta Blouin tract.*
>
> *Grandfather had a dairy farm on Perkins near Myrtledale. He also dug out the swamp and piled dirt on the side to make lots to sell. This was before the Civilian Conservative Corps* [CCC] *came out and dug the lakes in the thirties.*

The first house on University Lake in University Gardens was built by the late Berlin and Della Perkins, the parents of Verdie Reece Perkins. "It was on the corner of Ferndale and East Lakeshore," said Perkins. "My wife, Peggy, and I lived over thirty years across the street on the same corner." (Perkins and an uncle, V.R. Blake, bought the land for Hollydale Avenue, developing and building houses on it.)

Childhood memories of Naquin focus on the area lakes, including University and City Park Lakes. "All the kids in our neighborhood had little boats and motors," Naquin said. "We almost lived on the lakes. We put out fish traps and trotlines and fished all day. The island in the middle of University Lake, in the vicinity of the fraternity houses now, is gone. We'd build campfires, pitch tents and stay out there all night. I learned to water-ski in the lakes. I also took dates to LSU games by boat."

Naquin's parents built the brick house on Morning Glory in 1957. His grandparents, Julius and Mary Yunkes, built the house next door in 1944. A half-acre garden extended in the rear of both houses. "Grandfather grew early tomatoes," he recalled. "Staff members of the LSU Agriculture Department, impressed with the method and techniques he used to grow tomatoes, would visit. He started tomatoes from seed in a hothouse and one year, after taxes, made $5,000 from tomato sales, a lot of money then."

A licensed horticulturist and landscape contractor, Naquin landscaped the lawns of the French country design house, which he and his wife, Ann, bought from his parents in 1970. Renovating and expanding, they installed cypress beams from Orange Grove Plantation in West Baton Rouge, slate floors, brick walls, a large butler's pantry and old cypress cabinets. He also custom builds furniture.

A contrast is the towering stucco Mediterranean- and West Indies–inspired mansion fronting the lake at the corner of Ferndale and East Lakeshore. Located on the site where the V.R. Perkins family lived, it was built by attorney Frank Tomeny and his wife, Cathy. In July 2002, *Southern Living* magazine featured the courtyard and home. Steps lead down to a courtyard pool, with an outdoor fireplace and Jacuzzi. The home features a slate shingle roof, broad galleries, redwood louvers and shutters, French doors and an upper sleeping porch.

Baton Rouge native and portraitist Glen Nordyke Jr. has lived on East Lakeshore Drive since building his home in 1955. "My home, with St. Joseph brick, was one of the earlier Louisiana-style homes built in the area," he recalled, "and is typical of construction then." He added a studio and guesthouse to the three-bedroom, two-bath home. He likes the tranquility, the lake, ducks and wildlife and living near LSU.

Fascination with the area led Sanford and Corinne Lemoine to buy houses in the early 1970s. "We have five daughters and one son, and we bought six old homes out here," said Lemoine. "We started off doing this as an investment. When we realized this was a workable thing for family members, we continued. An old beat-up house would become available and we would get together as a family and fix it up, one house at a time. Then one of the kids would move in, or it would be a starter home after marriage." Two daughters still live in the area. The home of John and Nancy (Lemoine) Ellis on Morning Glory Avenue was featured in the magazine *This Old House* in October 2002. Nancy's sister, Anne Lemoine, lives on Stanford Avenue; her house was featured in a story by Carol Anne Blitzer in the *Advocate* on July 12, 1995.

John Ellis said they purchased their 1920s cottage in "a good kinfolk deal." They added 1,360 square feet to the existing 1,340. Family members, contractors and interior designers worked with them. A 4-foot-wide staircase, ballroom-size rooms and a great room featuring a fireplace and granite hearth enhance downstairs. The upstairs master bedroom has a fireplace, and the master bath has a Jacuzzi, shower and granite-top vanities. French doors open to a balcony overlooking Morning Glory Avenue. The large back gallery is a favorite place for family gatherings. The Ellises love the old trees, young and old families and the quietitude.

They can walk to the 1925 redwood house on Stanford Avenue owned by Anne Lemoine, who renovated the house after spending a year drawing up plans. "My father has done a lot for preservation with the houses he bought," she said. "He made it livable when he bought it in 1981. I did a major renovation in 1991, adding eight hundred square feet."

Leland Van Oss said that University Gardens "feels like home." Retired, he moved to Cedardale Avenue in 1958 when he married Libby Blanchard. "This is just a beautiful area," he said. "The houses are all different, young people move in and brighten up things, flowers are planted and trees replanted."

David and Patti Bruce Beste added a dining room onto their yellow cypress house with a circular driveway on Ferndale Avenue. They and their daughter, Camille, like being near the lake, a good place for runners, including David.

Some University Gardens residents pay dues to both the Southside Civic Association and the Lakeshore Civic Association, along with separate patrolling by off-duty police. The Southside Civic Association covers thirteen subdivisions, including Southdowns.

The Southside Civic Association supports the independently run Krewe of Southdowns Parade during Mardi Gras. "Our ongoing current focus is a detailing of the rental houses," said Richard Barker. "Old families die or move, and younger family members rent the houses. We are visiting each rental house in an effort to get a handle on this property. We have a stable, prominent, responsible neighborhood."

Lake beautification is the thrust of the Lakeshore Civic Association, headed by attorney George Bayhi, who lives on East Lakeshore on City Park Lake. "Our area encompasses homes facing the lake on East Lakeshore from Stanford to City Park Lake, including homes facing the golf course up to Perkins Road. We also take in some of the Hillsdale area, go along Dalrymple Drive and into the Lake Crest area (March, April, May, June and July Streets). The association got a $500 can-do grant from the mayor's office that allowed the installation of white plastic barrels with decals on City Park Lake."

Through time and generations, land was subdivided, subdivisions were made and families meshed. (See "A Premier Attraction Near City Park" for more information.)

Southdowns and Mardi Gras

World-traveled Lieutenant Colonel Philemon St. Amant said he would not want to live any place other than Southdowns. He remembered when the area was pasture and swampland.

Dr. Will Gladney, neurologist, said that Southdowns is "the center of the universe." When Gladney started the Krewe of Southdowns Parade during Mardi Gras season in 1988, the parade had half a dozen vehicles, the king rode on a golf cart and the queen rode in a sports car. Ten years later, the incorporated Krewe had fifty flambeaux carriers, twenty-five vehicles and marching bands and sixty thousand spectators.

What Southdowns possesses is an old-fashioned sentiment and neighborhood charm, from its modest homes to its fence-encircled mansions. Here, vintage homes and newer, sumptuous homes comingle. A strong civic association, Southside, and the annual parade evoke togetherness.

The umbrella civic association extends from Ferndale in University Gardens near Perkins Road Overpass through Southdowns itself from Hood to Glasgow, bounded by Perkins Road and Duplantier Swamp (Lee High area). Most property owners in Stanford Place are also included, said Bob Roland, a board member for thirty years. Off-duty police patrol the area.

When nonagenarian Augusta St. Amant Bradsher, the sister of St. Amant, moved into her cypress home with a screened porch and porte cochere on the corner of Hyacinth and Stuart, she was a teen bride. "I have lived here seventy-one years," she said. "My father had this house built while Dr. Bradsher and I were on our wedding trip to Europe." In 1927, at age nineteen, she married

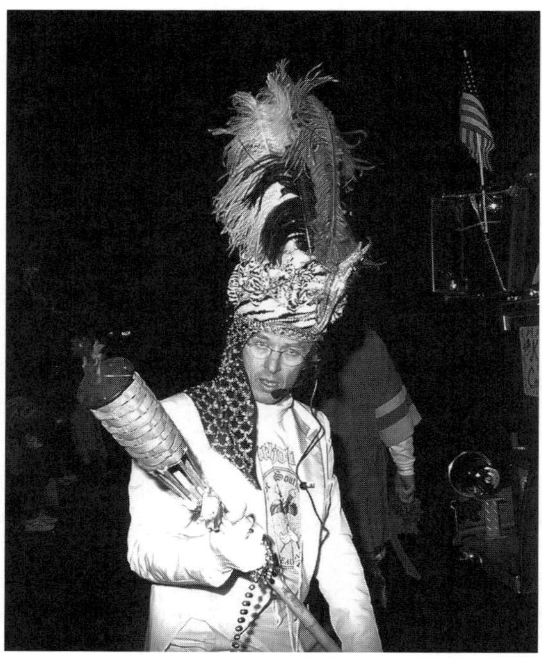

The spirited Southdowns Mardi Gras Parade was founded by Will Gladney in 1988, shown in 2002 as captain-flambeau carrier. *Photo by Greig Olivier.*

Bradsher, age forty-eight, an LSU professor. The garden wedding took place at her parents' home on twenty acres at the corner of Hyacinth Avenue and Knollwood Drive. The Bradshers had two sons, Henry and (the late) Earl Jr., and were happily wed until Bradsher's death at ninety-five in 1974.

The Bradshers renovated their house and cherished lawn and garden. "My husband planted the oaks and brought many of them from the swamp to our home and planted them, as well as the site that became Lee High School. We have a beautiful magnolia, and from my bedroom window, I can see a holly that is glorious in the fall, chock full of berries."

Alfred St. Amant, the father, developed Southdowns in 1923. "Our father and a silent partner developed Southdowns," said St. Amant, who remembered when the family home, built in 1925, burned down in February 1932. He was fourteen. Today, he resides with his wife, Corinne, on Stuart Avenue, named for Confederate general J.E.B. Stuart. Their house was built by his father in 1949; they added a great room in 1985. He retains old maps at his accounting office.

"Daddy purchased a large portion of Richland Plantation from a Judge Landry, and he sold the part now known as Meadowlea to Walter Brame. He named all the north and south streets for Confederate generals, including Lee, Pickett, Stuart, Hood, Stevens and Johnston (changed to Glasgow). The streets running east and west followed the ridge between drainage of Bayou Duplantier on the south and Dawson Creek on the north. Angled streets were named for trees. Later, other developers with a Scottish bent named Aberdeen and Glasgow."

"I grew up setting traps and killing alligators in Bayou Duplantier, then called Perkins Swamp. When I was seven I learned to swim in a pond on the Lee High campus. The swamp would overflow every spring when the Mississippi would rise, and it stayed a swamp until the late 1930s. Stanford Avenue was called Loop Road and was cut through in the early 1920s by Henry W. Jolly, connecting the areas now called College Town and University Gardens."

Nearby in Southdowns' oldest house, more than one hundred years old, is Kim Boudreaux, a chemical engineer at Albemarle Corp. Since 1984, she has lived in the two-bedroom stucco house with cypress interior walls and a front porch.

Also on Stuart is the Acadian-style two-story house of Gladney and his family. The twenty-year-old house was remodeled with old materials, including salvage pine flooring, cypress doors and accoutrements found in New Orleans. The lawn is like a park, studded with old trees and hundreds of camellias. Gladney is planting a variety of native trees and foliage to make a miniature arboretum. Arrowheads found on the property indicate the presence of Native American Indians. The screened tree house, with its iron staircase, towers fifty feet over the bayou tributary, and a sheep shed, more than one hundred years old, remains on the rear of the property with the original sugar kettles.

Meadow Lea Rolling with Memories

Meadow Lea Subdivision was once a private racetrack, stables and pastures for Tennessee walking horses owned by Gordon H. Brame. In 1956, Verdie Reece Perkins and Hal Phillips Sr. bought seventy-three acres from Brame. They began developing Meadow Lea in 1957. Brame Drive is the one entrance-exit into Meadow Lea, where Hyacinth Avenue ends.

With its lowland and hills, moss-hung cypress trees and wildlife, Meadow Lea is an off-the-beaten-track niche of natural beauty. Situated near a large lake and three ponds are houses that are personalized signatures on a landscape of diverse architectural designs, including those of French and Spanish origin.

"We had lot one and Meadow Lea had sixty-six lots when we developed it," said octogenarian Perkins. "My wife, Peggy, and I kept the lot 43 years but didn't build on it for 7, when we decided to sell our 175-year-old Santa Maria Plantation Home out Perkins Road and move onto Whitehaven Street." The

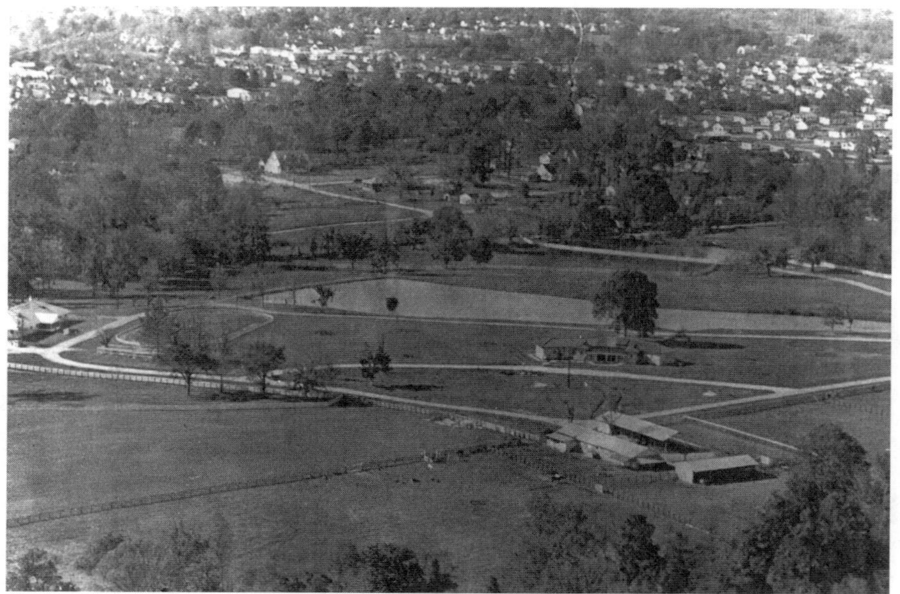

Prior to the Meadow Lea development, Gordon H. Brame had a private racetrack and stables for Tennessee walking horses. *Courtesy of Meadow Lea Civic Association.*

pigeonnaire at their home is patterned after one at Santa Maria, copied after a home in Washington, Louisiana.

Today, a Meadow Lea residential map shows additional houses and eighty-four lots. At the rear of the subdivision, land is measured in acres, not square feet.

Brame purchased eighty-six acres in 1945 from Harry B. Nelson, and in the next three years the land, located below what is now Southdowns, was cleared. From 1945 to 1956, Brame had a horse farm. In 1947, his stepson, Lea Johnson, designed and built the family home, the Brame House, on Belvedere Drive and Meadow Lea Lake. In 1958, the house was sold to Mr. and Mrs. Fred Hochenedel Jr.

"I was five years old when my parents bought the Brame House," said Fred Hochenedel III. "It was like living in the country. My father planted the pine trees for privacy."

His father owned businesses and sold real estate. After his father's death, his mother, Shirley, sold the home to the Farguson family and moved to a smaller home next door on East Bluebell Drive. His mother having moved to a retirement home now, Fred Hochenedel III and his wife, Dennise Carlisle, are renovating the brick and siding house to make room for their three school-age sons.

The neighboring Fargusons have lived in the Brame House since 1980. "We had central air and heat put in, improved the garden room and updated the baths and kitchen about twenty years ago when our family moved in," said Dr. Crayton Farguson, an opthamologist. "We wouldn't live anywhere but here. It's peaceful and we have good neighbors."

Ann LeBlanc Guercio grew up on Meadow Lea Drive and now lives with her husband, Rob, and two daughters on Belvedere Drive. "I have lived in Meadow Lea since I was five," she said. "I was in the eighth grade when we moved into this house. My father, a general contractor, bought the house as a shell and finished it in 1970."

The spacious house is located on a large pond that was dug out by her father and stocked by the late "Sleepy" McCarty. "All the houses out here are large and different, each unique," said Guercio. She recalled putting rabbits on leashes and walking them through Mildred Gladney's yard, where they ate the pansies. "She never said a word to us," Guercio added. "We see all kind of animal life—nutria, possums, raccoons, armadillos and, occasionally, foxes."

One of the first houses built belonged to Paul Dietzel, who coached the LSU Tigers from 1955 to 1961 and was athletic director from 1978 to 1982. "Once the Ole Miss fans drove through looking for Coach Dietzel's house so that they could egg it. When they couldn't find it, they egged everybody," Guercio said.

Guercio is longtime president of the loosely knit Meadow Lea Civic Association, which holds one annual meeting and numerous parties. "We have been chartered and had a board for twenty-five years," she said. "We have no dues. We meet once a year in 'the Hollow,' behind our house on the lake, or in 'the Pines' at the Brame House."

During Mardi Gras season were the children's parades. "At our first parade, Anne and Bob Stout, honorary grandparents of Meadow Lea, were king and queen," said Ann. "The children decorated their wagons, bicycles and tricycles. Also, Peter Bahlinger drove his red convertible at the end of the parade."

Bahlinger and his wife, Mary Claire Bonnet Bahlinger, moved into their home on their twelfth wedding anniversary, January 31, 1959. He is a fourth-generation Bahlinger in Baton Rouge. "Meadow Lea was open fields and had all kind of places for our children to play," he said, adding that he likes having steady neighbors and the one entrance-exit.

Where Streets Are Named for Flowers: Pollard Estates

The drilling of an oil well in Pollard Estates delayed its development, according to Miles Pollard, son of the late O.M. Pollard, developer. An LSU student when his father began the development in 1956, he later sold lots in the subdivision where the streets were named for flowers—the exception being Pollard Parkway.

"The timing was right for the development," said Pollard. "In the mid-1950s, many families who had bought homes after World War II in the Southdowns area were outgrowing them. People bought lots off the map before the streets were laid by Barber Brothers Contractors. "

Rosalie Strickland on South Dahlia Street said that she and her late husband, Neil, bought their house in 1960, when there were few houses on Pollard Parkway. She served as treasurer of the civic association for seven years and said she enjoys the serene neighborhood with many walkers and young parents strolling with their children.

Margaret Hannaman, who has lived for thirty-nine years on South Tamarix Avenue, recalled when her late husband, Bill, served on the association board for some twenty-five years and worked with the architectural control committee. "We had so many house plans that people never came back for that Bill and I drove every evening for a whole week to deliver them. I have the seventeen restrictions for those who built out here. We watched almost every house go up."

Long-term residents abound. Since 1971, Joan May, who worked for O.M. Pollard and is now executive assistant for Miles, has lived with her husband, Bill, on Dahlia Street.

Penny Nichol grew up here and bought her home from her parents, William Nichol and the late Sue Nichol. The homes of Nichol and adjacent houses are sited on the highest elevation, like a ridge, on the Parkway.

Pollard Estates has a special closeness. Like Jefferson Place/Bocage, many children reared here returned as adults to buy homes. "On any weekend, if we want to have friends around, we have any number we can phone to come over, barbecue hamburgers and watch our children play," said Buck Gladden III.

Dianne Guidry and her husband, Gil, who have always enjoyed living in South Baton Rouge, bought their house on South Pollard Parkway from First United Methodist Church and have had several renovations and landscaping done. Dianne's goal as president was to install a glass-enclosed fixture at the entrance, a place where residents may post notices.

To the rear of Pollard, developed in the late 1980s, is New Pollard, with some fifty houses. Among residents on Elmcrest Drive, a cul-de-sac, is the family of pediatric dentist Dr. Mark Garon and his wife, Donna. "We bought one of the first lots and were the last to build," said Donna. "It's a neat street. Everybody is close. We have activities for our children, and the moms have cooking exchanges on holidays."

Mark said he went to re-sod the middle ground of the cul-de-sac recently, preparatory to planting flowers, and in less than thirty minutes had four neighbors helping.

The civic association has security, newsletters and an annual picnic.

Pollard has good neighbors in Woodchase, entered through Pollard's gates, to the right. The newer, separate subdivision, Woodchase was developed in 1991 by Bob Breazeale Jr. and Hardy Swyers. It has its own civic association, subdivision restrictions and forty-three lots on sixty-six acres. "We hired the same security patrol as Pollard and modernized subdivision restrictions," said Breazeale.

A pocket subdivision, Cold Water Creek, is nearer Perkins Road with eleven lots and 4.2 acres, with the creek dividing it from Woodchase. Houses range from $300,000 to $400,000 and higher.

V. Patrick Bella, attorney, and his wife, Chris, bought the second lot in Woodchase and built their Acadian-style house in 1994. "We like the cul-de-sac," said Bella. "We block off the street, have jambalaya and races for the children in the fall and a crawfish boil in the spring."

An Area of Hidden Harmony: Stratford Place

The entrance gardens at the access to Stratford Place were designed and built by a longtime resident, nationally known butterfly scientist Dr. Gary Ross. Composed of six streets and 144 lots, Stratford Place is entered on Moss Side Lane, located off busy Perkins Road and is bordered by Concord Estates, Ward's Creek and Moss Side Lane.

Pre-interstate, Stratford Place was the vision of Jack Burk Sr. and his son, the junior Burk, who started the development in 1969. Building began in the early 1970s. The senior Burk, former co-owner of Bernard and Burk Civil Engineers, was the initiator and got friends to invest in the land and subdivision. Street names further the Revolutionary War street names in adjacent Concord Estates, built prior to Stratford. The name emanated from a Revolutionary War battle fought at Stratford, Connecticut.

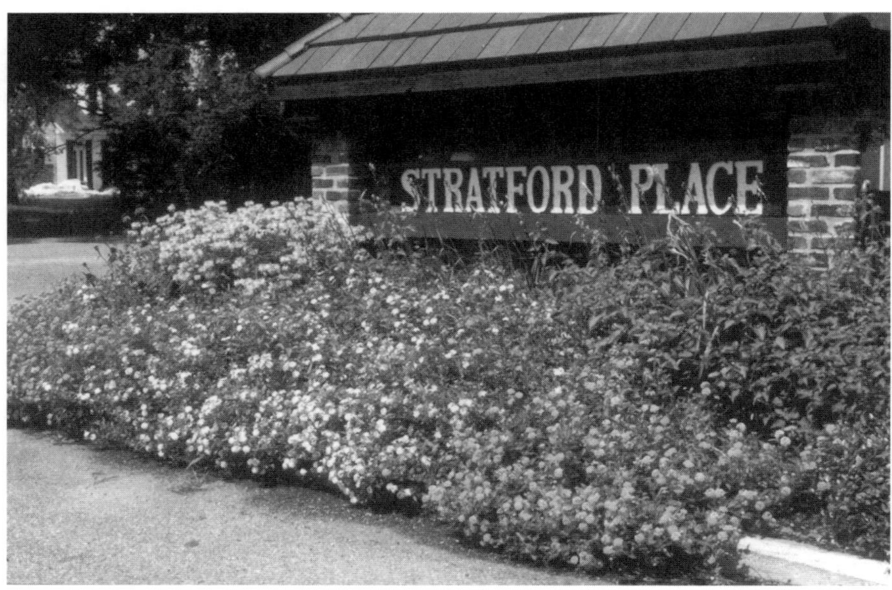

A pre-Katrina butterfly garden was part of a larger landscape that brightened the Stratford Place subdivision entrance. *Courtesy of Gary N. Ross.*

"Dad initially wanted no outlets on Moss Side Lane, but the City-Parish Planning Commission said that Stratford Avenue had to come out to Perkins Road," said the junior Burk. Besides the main entrance, it has entrances on two streets from Concord, Guilford and Bennington Avenues. The largest lots are along Stratford Avenue, averaging one-half to one acre each. "We purposely adjusted streets a little to avoid taking down a tree or two," said Burk. "We like nice trees." He also remembered having cattle there at one time.

One of the most integrated neighborhoods in Baton Rouge, Stratford Place has multiethnic professionals living harmoniously in homes appraised from $250,000 to $400,000.

Kathy Bishop said that "the area was a wilderness and Stratford Avenue had not been put all the way through when we moved in." She recalled a horse meandering through the dining room of her home when it was under construction in 1972. "It was real interesting," she said. She also recalled one spring when they first moved there when residents took to canoes after a drainage problem resulted from all the construction underway. This has not occurred since, she said.

"I remember when Shelby Guillory, a builder, was living out here, and one day his wife called to say she was scared to death. A man just walked by with a gun and rabbits," she told him. "I don't know what to do."

The red brick, two-story, five-thousand-square-foot-home of Dr. George and Kathy Bishop was on the Quota Club Open House Tour one year, and the couple were hosts at a neighborhood Christmas open house.

Pam Hutchinson, president of Stratford Place Homeowners Association, said about 60 percent of the residents are African American. Since 1992, she and Don Hutchinson and family have resided on Bennington Avenue, enjoying their 3,700-square-foot home and swimming pool. "It's very beautiful out here, and the people are neighborly and nice. The value of homes has gone up tremendously."

Hutchinson took part in the revitalization of the homeowners' association in 1997–98, after it had declined, and credited Eli Guillory as the activist in getting it going again. She took on the task of getting block captains and surveyed the area as to ages of families and the type of events they desired.

Guillory, an architect and facilities planner at Southern University, got homeowners to help clean up the entrance. "My wife, Karen, and I became friends with Bettye George, who told us the history of the subdivision and personally paid the utilities bill for the entrance and also held meetings at her home. We asked everyone to chip in and meet their neighbors."

Guillory said that he and Karen like their two-story Acadian-design house, the oak trees, atmosphere and harmony. "This is a neighborly, stabilized and very settled residential area," he said, "yet we have birds, rabbits, squirrels, raccoons from time to time and lots of butterflies."

Early residents include Dr. James D. and Anne McElveen, who built their brick A. Hays Town–designed home on Bennington Avenue and moved in on April 15, 1973. "We were the second ones back here," said McElveen, recalling that the Barfields' house was completed first. Thomas Atkinson Barfield and his wife, Julie, said their house was built in 1972, about the same time as the Bishops' and the McElveens'.

Cohesiveness is fostered by a strong homeowners' association, an electronic newsletter and a membership directory for computer-using residents. A summer-fest picnic and annual Christmas party are traditions.

A Country Place inside the City: Greenbriar Hollow

Sheltering oaks and crape myrtles planned by the homeowners' association line the grand entrance to Greenbriar Hollow Subdivision on Perkins Road just past Bluebonnet Road. On its north side is a ten-acre, tree-studded park adjacent to First Baptist Church Family Life Center, home also to Mission Church on Perkins.

Greenbriar Hollow Road, the entry, is one-quarter of a mile long, perfect for runners. On its south side, a high fence separates the subdivision from Oakridge subdivision. Sid Brian, Oakridge developer, also did the second filing of Greenbriar Hollow and required Oakridge dwellers at the rear to build the board fence and brick columns. Brian provided landscaping and entrance signs.

The first filing was for 107 homes in 1984 by attorney Craig Smith and retired contractor Ed McKnight, who bought twenty-five acres from developer Carl Clayton, with Ron Ferris as engineer. Brian developed the second filing in 1994, mostly along O'Brien Avenue, a name with an Irish tenor like many streets. Smith named three streets for his children: Patrick Drive, Leigh Ellen Avenue and Erin Vale Avenue.

The single- and two-story homes vary from 1,100 to 2,000 square feet. Corner lots are larger than the average 55- by 150-foot lots. Tidy, with picket fences, wrought-iron gates, patios and landscaping, Greenbriar has a contemporary look. The brick and stucco homes, with wood or siding, had different architects and builders but present a blended diversity.

Kurt and Stephanie Schroeck have lived here since 1985. "Our house was a year old, and there weren't that many houses out here then," said Stephanie. "The subdivision was developed about 1984. There were horses and pasture across Perkins Road, and no homeowners' association until 1994."

A runner, Stephanie wends from home to Perkins Road, through Oakridge and Oak Hills subdivisions, back to Highland Road and then home again. "It's about five miles, and I run it five times a week," she said.

She and Kurt agreed that their 1,700-square-foot, Acadian-style house with blue siding suits them to a T. "I walked in, saw it, said 'this is the house I want—period,'" she said.

Her mother, LaVeta Jones, widowed, resides on McShay Avenue, also in Greenbriar Hollow, and enjoys a single-story 1,700-square-foot home of brick and stucco with hardwood floors, some carpets, three bedrooms and two baths. She uses the boat port attached to the carport for added storage.

Another happy resident is Virginia Evans Carradine, widowed, who downsized from a larger home to the 1,500-square-foot home that has all the festures she desires. "Some evenings the neighbors and I sit outside and visit. We keep an eye out for each other. Some of us work, and some don't. I like having young children running around."

Carradine moved with her family to Baton Rouge when the town had forty thousand residents and she was a junior at Baton Rouge High School. "I was standing in the school cafeteria when Roosevelt declared World War II," she recalled. She finished Spencer Business College and went to work at the Industrial USO on Plank Road at a time when nine thousand industrial workers were living in trailer parks near the plants. She worked there until the war ended. Carradine has been active in the community and served as vice-president of the homeowners' association.

The association has occasional newsletters and burglary alerts, and its dues are used to maintain the landscape in a subdivision that maintains its country aura within the city.

Oakridge and Sense of History

Oakridge subdivision is named for its ridge of oaks that are loved and cared for by subdivision residents through an active homeowners' association. Located off Perkins Road just past Bluebonnet Drive, the subdivision entrance reflects its historic ties; the rear has a neighborhood park.

Great Oak Drive, entrance, was part of pastureland until its development and is marked by a common area with an ancient live oak tree, a wooden, freestanding swing and an old cistern that is evidence of the circa 1800 cypress house that had to be demolished prior to the development. The first filing documented was in December 1993.

Landscape architect Jon Emerson designed the entrance around the tree, and developer-environmentalist Sid Brian donated the common area to the homeowners' association. "Everyone who drove by this spot on Perkins Road remembers that old house," he said.

Linda Fletcher recalled staying in the old family home, built in the 1800s, with her grandparents, Allen and Lucille Duval Richard. Her mother, Edna Mae Richard Fletcher, only child of the Richards, grew up there. "We kept the windows wide open, as there was no air conditioning," she said. "Perkins was a dirt road, and when we heard a car coming, it was coming to visit us or two other families."

Brian Development purchased the land from the late Edna Mae Richard Fletcher and called her "a great lady."

"Oakridge's rules were made to maintain the former environment. Every homeowner was required to plant a native hardwood tree in the front yard, in conjunction with Baton Rouge Green, and mandates included a designated mailbox, annual fees, landscaping and building items."

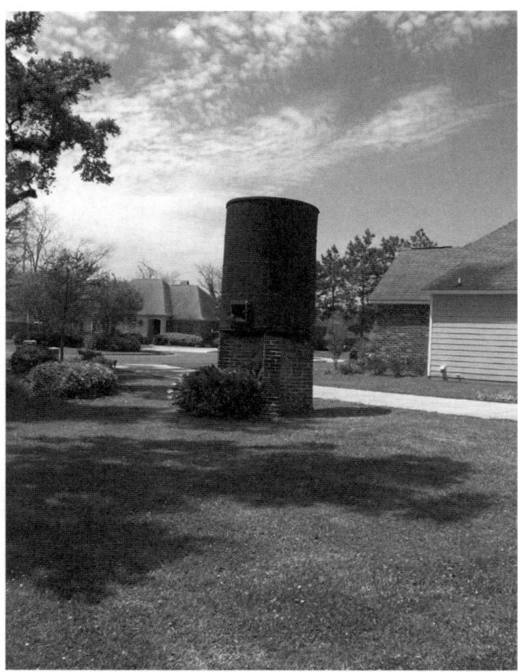

Sid Brian donated property at the Oakridge entrance to the homeowners' association. An old cistern is one reminder of the past.

Brian was in partnership with John Barton Sr. and John Barton Jr. for the first three filings, on land bought from Fletcher. The fourth filing, Plantation Oaks Drive, was developed by John H. Fetzer III and Hardy Swyers on land purchased from the Shelvin family and completed in December 1996. These developers sold six acres at cost to the Recreation and Park Commission of East Baton Rouge Parish for Rue LeBouef Park.

The first house was built on Great Oak Drive for Dr. Wanjun Wang, an LSU professor of engineering, and his wife, Dr. Yushen Lee, a family medicine physician. Both were born, educated and married in China, and they have three children. The expanse of windows that reflect the outdoors and their large, solid oak kitchen, as both like to cook, were attractions. "We're only fifteen minutes away from LSU," said Wang.

Scott Jolly, association president and attorney, his wife, Nancy, and their two children love walking to the park. They reside on a dead-end street across from the park where the association has its annual picnic. Their home was a spec house built by their former neighbor in Kenilworth, Ted Nissing, and they enjoy the mother-in-law suite. "We have a place for family and guests, separate from the rest of the house, affording privacy to our overnight guests," he said.

He credited David Monett, past association president, with laying the groundwork for the strong association, a cross-section of ages. "We all get along famously."

"Our neighborhood grows babies like crazy," said resident Jack Klopf, Albemarle Corp. retiree. He and Mary have two grown children. "We bought our lot first and two years later had our house built. We used to hike out here in boots when it was pastureland. We would watch the horses, look at the terrain and figure out what we wanted." Their brick, stucco and wood house is Country French design.

"Being with younger couples with children really keeps us going," stated Bonnie LeBoeuf, whose late husband, Harry, served on the association's first board of directors. Also a former board member, she loves her "very caring neighborhood." "I will never forget the blood drive the subdivision had for my husband. There was a fantastic turnout." He died of leukemia in June 2001. She cherishes her home ("it's very serene"), especially the rear patio, constructed of New Orleans brick, with a wrought fence.

"The location of Oakridge is ideal," she added. "I'm close to my bank, the Bluebonnet library, St. George Church and Calandro's Grocery."

The active association has a board of directors, annual picnic and meeting and a newsletter, *The Acorn*.

Wimbledon and the Tennis Greats

Carved from Kleinpeter family pastureland, Wimbledon Estates is a tribute to tennis greats and was intended to be a tennis community. Located off Perkins Road just south of Bluebonnet Road, Wimbledon Estates was begun in 1974 by Van B. Calhoun Jr. of Springfield and Thomas A. Nolan of Baton Rouge.

"The Wimbledon partnership acquired 365 acres in 1973 from the Edward Kleinpeter estate and started construction in late 1974," said Calhoun, who lives on the Tickfaw River. "Edward Kleinpeter was my uncle. The property was part of the original Gertrude Kleinpeter estate that extended back to Jefferson Terrace and Jefferson Highway. There are many Kleinpeters, all of whom go back to an 1,800-acre Spanish land grant in 1786."

Also off Perkins Road is Oak Hills Crossing, carved from property of a Kleinpeter relative, Robert Lee Kleinpeter Jr., owner of adjacent acreage.

Wimbledon Estate itself was 180 to 200 acres and went across the Kansas City Southern Railroad track to what is now part of the Mall of Louisiana. "We had an oil well back there, which we named Wimbledon I," said Calhoun.

Plans for the tennis community failed when interest rates climbed to 18 to 21 percent in 1979–80, Calhoun said. "We held on as long as we could and then sold land to various other individuals. Before the community was

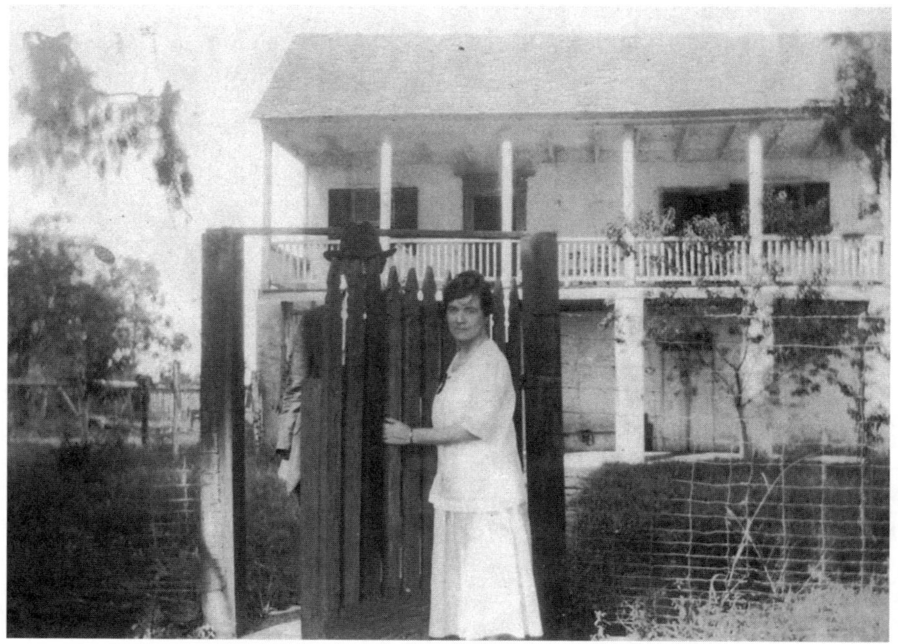

In 1920, Gertrude Kleinpeter poses at the circa 1820 Kleinpeter home, now located at the Settlement at Willow Grove. *Courtesy of Laurie Kleinpeter Laville.*

fully developed, we turned it over to a local bank and they sold it to another developer, Rick Hartley, who finished it."

Dunham School, on Roy Emerson Drive at the rear of Wimbledon, utilizes the building originally meant to be a tennis club. Extensive renovations and additions enhance the private school, which Chris Tuminello, president of Wimbledon Estates Civic Association, called "a good neighbor."

Calhoun and Nolan came up with the tennis street names. "In the mid-1970s, Bobby Riggs came to town and played a match with former Governor Edwin Edwards, and we had our grand presentation for Wimbledon at the Hilton the day after the Riggs-Edward tournament," he recalled.

The name is derived from Wimbledon, a suburb of London, England, and the historic site of the unofficial world championship for men's and women's singles and doubles held every summer. Wimbledon streets include Wimbledon Avenue and streets named for professional tennis players, including Baton Rouge's Hamilton "Ham" Farrar Richardson, a University High graduate who won national championships and was voted into several tennis halls of fame. Also included are tennis greats Rod Laver, Chris Evert,

Lew Hoad, Roy Emerson, John Newcombe, Don Budge, Maureen Connolly, Neal Fraser and Jack Kramer. A cul-de-sac is named for Margaret Smith, plus there are thoroughfares named Center Court and Back Court.

With small rolling hills and pristine homes, the average lot being 100 by 150 feet, Wimbledon has 174 homes. It retains its crisp, new appeal with no sign of litter. Developed in the late 1970s and early 1980s, Wimbledon has two exit/entrances, each off Perkins Road.

The civic association is led by Tuminello, who has served several years. His 2,700-square-foot brick home on Don Budge Avenue, built in 1982, is on an elevated site and has a front porch, as do many homes here. "We have an ethnic neighborhood, with residents with ties to LSU and Southern, and our architecture is diverse, with Acadian and contemporary styles," he said.

Even though the tennis community did not come into being, Wimbledon still has excellent tennis players. Michael Carpenter was one of the top ten tennis players in Canada before being transferred here from Toronto, Ontario, Canada, with Ethyl Corp., now Albemarle Corp. He and his wife, Joyce, play tennis at Bocage Racquet Club and reside on Lew Hoad Avenue.

Harvey Honore Jr., a contractor, built houses in Wimbledon and served as president of the architectural committee at the outset. "We approved plans for any houses planned in our area, saw that each had the minimum requirement, 2,250 square feet living area space and met the criteria appearance wise. I remember we rejected plans for a proposed dome-type house in Wimbledon."

Residents tout the location and its closeness to the Mall of Louisiana and the BREC Highland Road Park, which has twelve courts. They enjoy daily patrol by a sheriff's deputy.

Monet-Inspired: Oakbrook

Decks, bridges and walking trails add to the rusticity of Oakbrook subdivision, off Perkins Road between Bluebonnet Boulevard and Siegen Lane. Developed in 1973 by John Wiese and Larry Sleeth, the land was purchased from the heirs of Louis B. Kleinpeter and was once part of the Kleinpeter Spanish land grant going back to 1786. Here, historic trees and widely spaced homes, some built by Wiese and Sleeth, are complemented by a two-acre lake featuring bridges, fountains and lighting installed by the civic association.

Oakbrook's walking path around the lake encompasses most of the neighborhood, accessible by one entrance, Oakbrook Drive, which turns onto

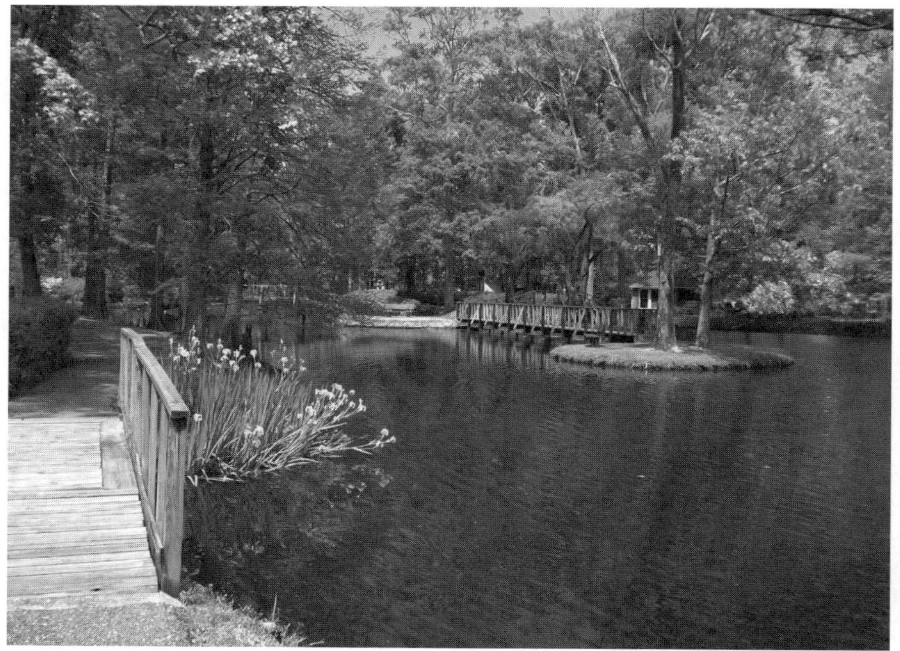

A two-acre lake with lighted fountains, decks, bridges and walking trails lends the aura of a peaceful, wooded retreat to Oakbrook subdivision.

Oak Hollow Drive and Oak Shadow Avenue. Some forty-two homeowners of different ethnic backgrounds live on sixty-three acres in diverse style houses. Lots range from three-quarters of an acre to seven-plus acres.

A park protects and encloses the remnant of a cemetery that has ties with the Kleinpeter family and is still a subject of interest as to the exact persons interred there. Wiese, interested in the history, pointed to an old well and the site of a now-gone Kleinpeter house.

"We have beautiful old oaks on our common property that our annual dues help maintain," said Staci Duhe, Oakbrook Civic Association president. Residents plan special events for the children and hold a yearly crawfish boil, holiday parties and cleanup days.

Craig and Staci Duhe built their brick and stucco home of French influence in 1990 on a lot just under an acre. Community leaders active in their three children's lives, they added on a game room, office and outdoor area. Fronting the entrance courtyard is an oak registered by the Louisiana Live Oak Society.

The year they married, 1988, Staci started a business, Nursing Care Connections, with Betty Bowers, an RN. The business was her response to a diving accident sustained by her brother, Sloan. After Craig joined the company, Staci became a full-time homemaker and community volunteer. "We love living near family," said Staci, whose parents, Norman and Kay Deumite, and brothers, Sloan and Scott, reside in Oakbrook.

Oakbrook had half the residents it now has when Kay and Norman Deumite, wed in 1961, moved into their contemporary ranch home on July 4, 1979. They designed the home with the help of a draftsman and built it on one and three-quarters of an acre. Old St. Joe brick from the Coca-Cola Bottling Plant in downtown Baton Rouge was used. "I persuaded Sherman Griffin, a superb bricklayer, to come out of retirement to do the work, his last job," said Norman. "He told me that one of his first jobs was laying these same bricks for the old Coca-Cola plant downtown, that was torn down."

The Deumites' great room has a twenty-five-foot ceiling and glassed vista of the pool and outdoor terrain. Diverse trees include white, red and live oaks, pecan, cypress, black walnut and magnolias. A stream feeds into Ward's Creek. Wildlife they have seen includes a blue heron, owls, possums, raccoons, squirrels and egrets in a cypress tree.

The increase of young families thrills the civic activists, who established a scholarship at Catholic High School in memory of their son, Steven, killed in an accident in 1979. Deumite started his own company, Industrial Maintenance, in 1971, and his sons, Scott and Sloan Deumite, work with him.

Another early Oakbrook resident, Dorothy Willis, lives on almost seven and a half acres of the lush, natural landscape in a fence-enclosed, two-story Acadian-style home built in 1978. "At that time there were about twenty homes in here."

Retired from LSU are Art and Norma Roberts, who bought their lot in 1974, started building in 1978 and moved in on Mardi Gras 1979. "We practically live outside," said Art, who took a landscape gardening course from Neil Odenwald and then became a master gardener. He has landscaped throughout Oakbrook's common grounds, helped put in Louisiana irises and daylilies and built a bridge. Their contemporary house has glass expanses overlooking the pool and lake.

Bernard and Betty Berry came to Baton Rouge from Mississippi in 1961, when Bernard started work as a chemical engineer for Ethyl Corp., now Albemarle. Their house of old brick and redwood, built in 1976, is angled on two acres, facing the lake. "Living here fits our lifestyle," said Betty. "Bernard is a bird-watcher and nature lover." With neighbors Charles and Carol White, they had a pond dug in 1983, and Bernard built a wooden bridge in his workshop to span the pond that Bernard labeled as the White-Berry Pond. Attorney Charles White rolled the bridge into place. Of the view, Carol White described it as "Monet-inspired."

Their California contemporary home has views of water from almost every room. Charles wrote deed restrictions for the adjacent Paula Manship YMCA that enabled residents and the Y to live and work in cohesiveness.

SISTER SUBDIVISIONS AUDUBON TERRACE AND MORNING GLEN

Audubon Terrace and Morning Glen subdivisions sit quietly near one of East Baton Rouge Parish's busiest intersections, Siegen Lane and Interstate 10—accessible off Perkins Road and directly across from the Siegen Marketplace. Traffic hums where Siegen exits onto Kinglet Drive, the only way in or out of the subdivisions, with two-hundred-plus households. It wasn't always this way. Many remember when this was still country.

Dramatic changes underway, including construction of a service road between Bluebonnet Boulevard (the Mall of Louisiana) and Siegen Lane, have not altered the tranquillity.

Built on property once part of a 1786 Spanish land grant to the Kleinpeter family, as was St. George Catholic Church, both subdivisions enjoy a sense of community. "We're one big happy family that pulls together," said Robin Hote, president of the Audubon Terrace/Morning Glen Homeowners Association since 1994.

The first filing of Audubon Terrace, encompassing Kinglet, Goldfinch, Thrush and Bunting Drives, was developed by Terrace Land Co., a partnership made up of Robert Lee and Ben Kleinpeter, C.E. Metrailer Sr. and Pat Alexander. Terrace Land bought the land in 1958 and developed Audubon Terrace in 1960. In 1972, the Metrailer family bought out other shareholders and developed the second part of the subdivision, extending Kinglet and Bunting and added the cross-street, Tanager.

The sister subdivision, Morning Glen, was developed by Cameron-Brown South, a Delaware trading company that bought the land from the heirs of Louis B. Kleinpeter. Morning Glen includes Buttercup, Hawthorne and Mint Drives. Morning Glen was developed on February 4, 1977, per the subdivision restrictions and building conditions.

Albert E. Ellis Jr. recalled that Siegen Lane was blacktop surrounded by pastureland and wooded areas when he and Mildred built their home

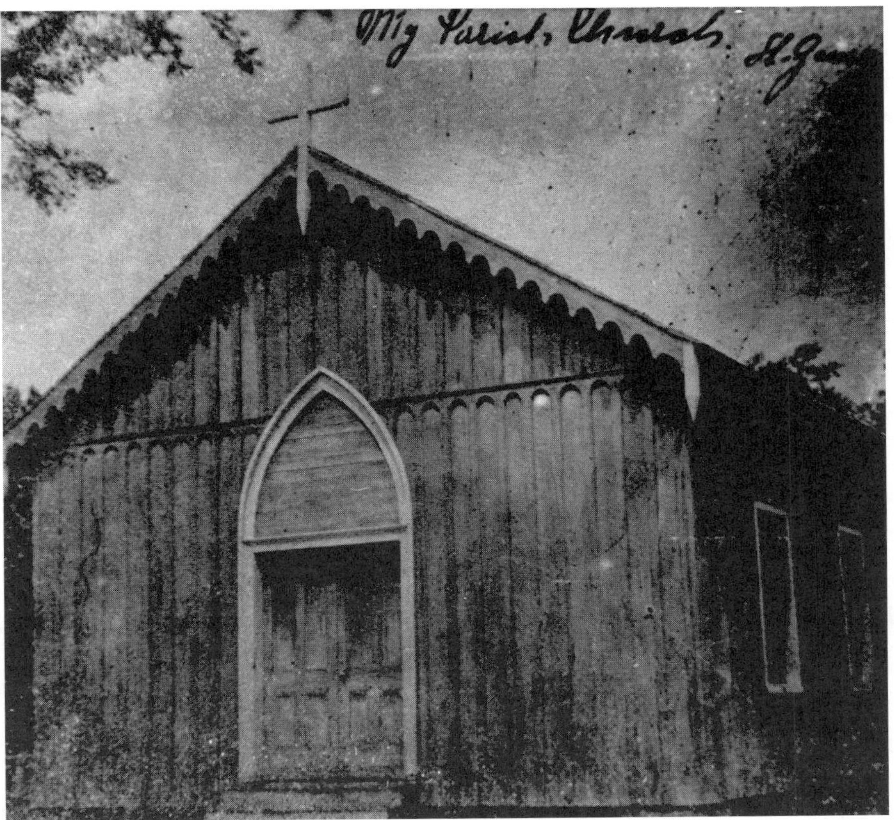

St. George Catholic Church, shown in 1888, and present-day Audubon Terrace and Morning Glen subdivisions were on Kleinpeter land. *Courtesy of St. George Church.*

in Audubon Terrace. "We bought our lot for three-quarters of an acre for $1,500, told my brother-in-law, architect Fred Dupre, what we wanted and Roy Schnebelen built our home for about $16,000. It was inexpensive and so very country. St. George Church was here, the children had plenty of places to play and we liked our neighbors."

Frank and Velta Simon Marabella built their home in Audubon Terrace in 1966 when there were no more than ten houses there, according to Frank. "Our son Frankie was three years old, and we wanted him to be able to walk to school." They bought their large corner lot for $3,600, and J.C. Patin built the four-bedroom, two-and-a-half-bath house for $23,000.

When James and Jeannette Simon Wax moved near the Marabellas, they had good reason. "Velta was my only sister, and I wanted to help her care for our elderly parents who lived nearby in Audubon Terrace." The Waxes installed a swimming pool and renovated their two-bedroom brick home over the years.

Also big on renovating are Charles and Theresa Champagne Rivault, who built their house in 1964. "I wanted subdivision living and Charles wanted country, so we compromised," said Theresa. "Our house was custom-built by Wayne Hirschey." Wed in 1960, they saw their children walk to St. George School and contemplated moving after the children were grown but, instead, improved and redid their backyard.

In 1992, when Patricia Oliver bought her home on Kinglet Drive, she was single. Now married to Robert Hall, she said, "Shortly after came Wal-Mart in Siegen Village, Siegen was four-laned and the overpass built. Siegen is now seven lanes. We've had a lot of neighborhood meetings due to zoning battles and are a strong community."

In neighboring Morning Glen, Robin Hote, president of the homeowners' association, said she bought her brick house in April 1989 for $42,000. "I take the interstate to work. It's only twelve miles from my carport to the parking lot behind the Capitol Annex." She got involved with the association after walking house to house with a petition for the city parish to dig out the servitude ditch of Ward's Creek behind her home and others. "We normally have annual meetings, and I send several newsletters a year. When something comes up, I send out more and get support at the drop of a hat."

Following Historic Highland Road

Once Daigre Family Farmland: University Hills

University Hills off Highland Road, within walking distance of LSU, was once part of the large farm of the Denis Daigre family. Hundreds of acres extended from the present-day south gates of LSU past Lee Drive and also included what are now College Town and Plantation Trace subdivisions. The subdivision of two-hundred-plus homes is laced with centennial oaks and winding, sloping thoroughfares overlaid with leaves that lend a small-town aura. Complete with wildflowers and shaded naturalness, the result is a charming park setting.

Almost all streets are named for colleges and universities, with a few later changes, such as Louisiana to Delgado Drive and Ursuline to Jefferson Drive. Its widely varied architecture ranges from a towering French chateau some call a castle to a secluded, end-of-the-road, one-thousand-square-foot cottage with a front screened porch.

For nearly thirty years, Dr. Eugene and Jeanne Tims lived here, but they sold their home recently to move to Camelia Trace. They helped form the civic association when asked by M. Clyde Day, a retired LSU chemistry professor, who served some twenty-five years as association president. The home he shares with his artist wife, Van Wade-Day, on Druid Circle backs up to Bayou Duplantier.

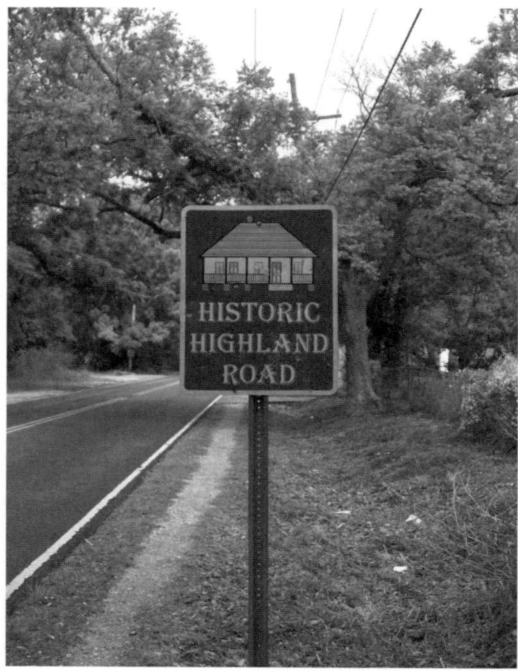

Historic Highland Road near the Mississippi River was the south entrance to Baton Rouge during the Civil War.

The Timses have a copy of the engineering plan for University Hills dated 1934, as laid out by A.G. Seifried of New Orleans, noting that it belonged to the Daigre estate.

Tims and a friend in industrial technology handcarved the large cypress entrance signs to University Hills and rewired the two lamp fixtures with concrete posts at the entry points.

When the city-parish attempted to buy the two-foot strip separating University Hills from Plantation Trace in order to build a street through to Tulane Drive in 1973, the civic association was highly motivated to organize. "Mr. Seifried was called and agreed to sell us the strip for $800," said Jeanne Tims. "Each resident invested about $15, and it now belongs to the residents."

In a separate story, Jane Duplantier Kelley remembered the Daigre farm days well. Her home, the Oaks on Highland Road, was the Daigre family home until her father bought it from his grandmother for the Duplantier family. Isabelle Daigre Duke sold her part that became University Hills to Augusta Pardue, whose nephew, Charles G. McDonald, brought in the gravel for Newcomb Drive, where he lived, part of the original development. McDonald purchased seven of his aunt's lots and made Newcomb part of the original development.

"Aunt Augusta was an unusual woman," said Mary McDonald. "She had a twin brother, August. Between 1926 and 1928, she bought the property, got a few family members to invest and developed University Hills. I doubt many women did that then."

Art critic for the *Advocate*, Anne Price recalled that she and her husband, Ed, copy editor, bought their family home to be close to work downtown from Mr. and Mrs. Norman Lant, who built the two-story brick in the late 1920s and completed it in 1930. Lant was chief engineer of the Louisiana Highway Department, and the house was one of the first built in the neighborhood. They later bought adjoining lots, making a total of four.

She treasures Lant's diary, a gift from a friend. "It shows how cheap things were during the Depression," said Anne, "with little notations like, 'A man came today to plant trees and was paid two dollars.'" When they moved in, the Prices had four children, and they had two more later. "A wonderful place for our children to grow up." She said, "They played in the woods all day in the summer, picked blackberries and sold them to neighbors. They had a huge game of hide-and-seek, with every child in the neighborhood playing."

Noel Hammatt, LSU clinical faculty member and school board member, likes the area, its history and their view. He grew up on nearby Mount Hope Plantation, where his family lived for one hundred years and he lived until he was fifteen.

> *When we bought our 1949 house, it needed a lot of work but was affordable. I did all of the work myself, including electrical. We added a master bedroom and bath.*
>
> *We enjoy the families that vary from wealthy to hourly wage earners, and the different types of houses. We like the Bicentennial Oak in the median that we can see from our front porch.*

Members of the media and LSU professionals are drawn to the area, as evidenced by the roster of residents.

The civic association remains one of the strongest in the area, paying particular attention to its residents and property.

Bayou Duplantier and Rolling Terrain: Plantation Trace

Duplantier Boulevard leads into Plantation Trace, a subdivision off Highland Road once part of Duplantier family property that backs up to Bayou Duplantier. The homes of cedar, brick, stucco and other materials in varying architectural styles were built to blend into the rolling hills and bayou floodline. Some split levels have decks overlooking wooded areas and the bayou.

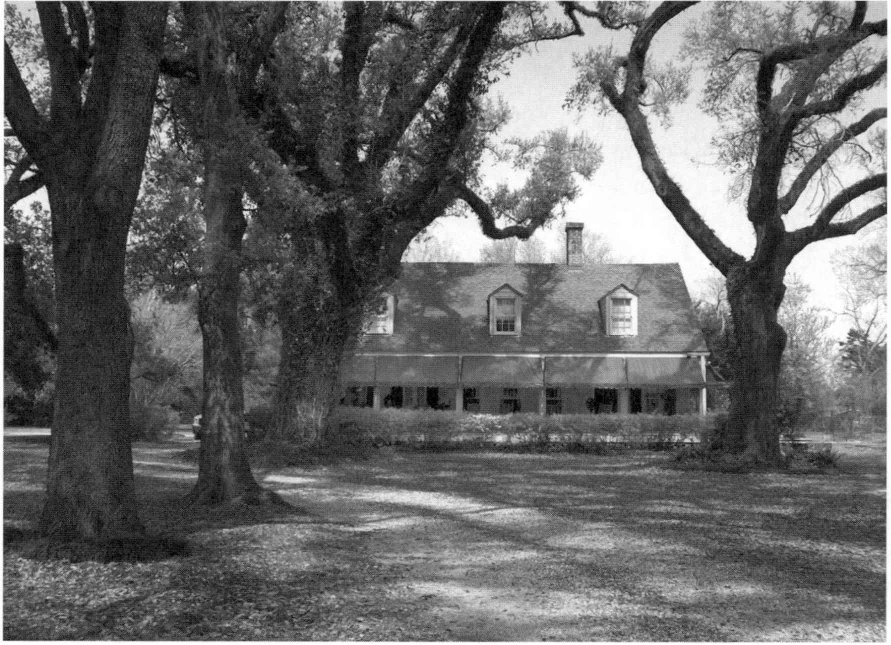

The Oaks was built some 170 years ago by Mr. and Mrs. Denis Daigre of the Duplantier family.

The boulevard is the one entrance-exit for the two-hundred-plus home subdivision, originally developed by Buddy Eanes and Robert Magill, starting in 1964 after purchase of the land in 1963. Seven homes were built, but hard economic times effected a delay of the development until 1971, when other developers took over. Most houses were built in the mid-1970s, but more filings followed.

The tranquility belies the fact that traffic flows on nearby Lee Drive and Highland Road. During the first filing, Dan Derbes sold houses for Eanes and Magill. "I remember the oil wells," he said. "When the streets were being cut through by Barber Brothers, Fred Matthews was on a road grader and ran across a gas line. It blew him off the machine."

The subdivision's first house on Brookhaven Drive, built in 1965, was home to Brad and Kathryn LeRay. Brad said:

> *We moved here to be close to LSU. First, we decided what lot we wanted and bought it, and we love our two-story brick home. We had children going to the university, wearing out automobiles.*

> *The boulevard was a dirt road. The builders had no electricity and no water in the subdivision. The city would not allow them to continue construction until they checked water lines under the house to ensure it was not leaking. When Buddy Eanes built our house and lived nearby, he had a bunch of hoses hooked up to his house. They would pull a generator with electric tools up into the driveway.*

He remembered picking blackberries for Kathryn to make "delicious pies."

In the second filing in a brick house on Glenburnie Drive completed in 1972, Bill and Ruth Patton Firesheets enjoy the peace and quiet. "It took us nine months to get the lot," he recalled. Bill drew the plans and subcontracted the work. The house with four bedrooms and two and a half baths was the right size for their family.

A striking and unusual setting goes with the scenic, two-story cedar siding home of State Representative Carl and Nancy Crane, built to go with the landscape. The Cranes moved into their house on Bancroft Way in 1977. "Three houses were going up in the circle at the same time," he said.

The lot swoops down into the Bayou Duplantier floodline. On the high part, the house is approached over a bridge. Decks were built to overlook the floodline. A foundation is twenty-five poured concrete shafts fifteen feet in the ground, with a gray beam on top and, on top of that, a nine-foot concrete brick wall and the house. Crane subcontracted the work.

All property owners become members of the Plantation Trace Residents Association, which was established in 1969 as a tax-exempt corporation. It has six board members. Among other things, the dues are used to maintain the lighting and sprinkler systems on the boulevard median and sponsor an annual meeting and Christmas party.

Driving though Plantation Trace is a scenic, historic experience. Residents in the area include descendants of Armand Allard Joseph Duplantier (1753–1827), who lived with his wife, Constance Rochon Joyce, at Magnolia Mound Plantation House on Nicholson Drive for thirty years. Duplantier came from France to America as an aide to Marquis de Lafayette and fought in the American Revolution.

Descendants include Denis Duplantier III and Curt Kelley on Highland Road across from the subdivision. They recall happy days of riding horses, hunting, picking berries and playing on the Daigre farmland before it became Plantation Trace.

"Until the end of the Depression, we had everything on our farm," said Curt Kelley. "My grandfather died in 1939, and after that, we had cattle and farmland. In 1953, there were no more row crops." He also remembered oil wells, still there when he was a child, part of the university field. "There was a blowout on one well that scared the heck out of all of us."

When she died in 2000, Jane Duplantier Kelley was making her home at the Oaks, 4979 Highland Road, her birthplace, not far from Plantation Trace's entrance. The Oaks was built some 170 years ago by Mr. and Mrs. Denis Daigre. Kelley said that her father, Denis Duplantier, bought the property from his mother, Clara Daigre Duplantier. She and her late husband, Richard Kelley, had resided in Plantation Trace prior to her move to the Oaks.

Home to Tradition: University Acres

University Acres residents keep home alive with action and words. They add to the hundreds of flowering cherry trees planted in the 1960s. They also continue a tradition begun during World War II—a coffee club formed by women that has long been open to all residents.

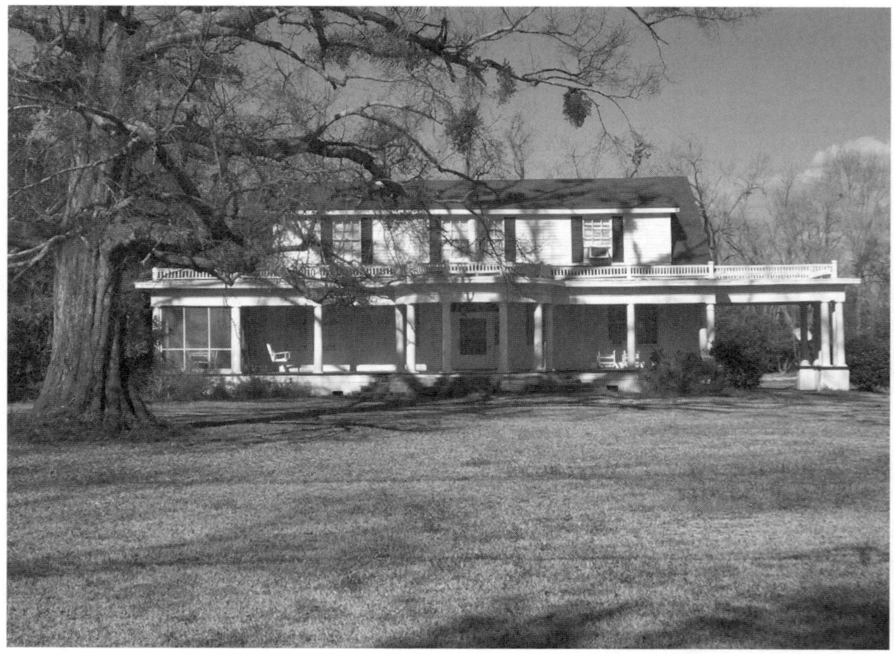

Since 1960, Bob and Nancy Claitor have lived at 5925 Highland Road, the former China Grove Plantation Home, a Union sanctuary during the Civil War.

Carved from China Grove, a three-hundred-acre cotton plantation owned by the Sam McConnell family, "the Acres" was developed in 1923 off Highland Road, a little more than one mile south of LSU. Bob and Nancy Claitor bought the plantation home in 1960 from American Bank and reared four sons here. China Grove was originally a Spanish land grant named for its chinaberry trees. During the Civil War, Union general Benjamin Butler used it as a sanctuary.

The name "University Acres" is fitting. Unlike most subdivisions, the homeowners prefer to keep the rolling acres rather than to sell and subdivide. It makes for a blend of regal homes and pastoral cottages. Complementing the mansions, like the antebellum home of Mike Wampold on Sunset Boulevard where a movie with George C. Scott Jr. was filmed, are small homes with pastoral settings like that of the artist Bill Stracener on Nelson Drive, where friendly goats wander about the yard.

The late Steele Burden, landscape architect–philanthropist, gave his talents generously to friends in University Acres. "Beautification is high on the list of priorities," said Stephen Creed, president of University Acres Civic Association, including in his praise of officers the beautification chairwoman Mag Wall.

"You don't want to miss springtime in the Acres," said Julia Hawkins, who has lived on Boone Drive over fifty years.

Since its original development in 1923, along with College Town and University Hills, the subdivision has stayed a favorite place for LSU employees. Although the campus was not officially moved from the state capitol/Pentagon Barracks area to its present location until 1925, some structures were underway or completed in 1923.

Harry B. Nelson, a real estate and oil man, bought the land from Berlin Perkins, sold lots and further developed it, renaming some streets. "Nelson was a good friend of my father's," said Verdie Reece Perkins, realtor. "The Harry B. Nelson Memorial Building at LSU was named for him."

A small stone marker in the ground near the cypress sign at the Sunset Boulevard entrance is a tribute to the late William F. Burbank, dubbed the unofficial mayor of University Acres and for whom Burbank Drive is named.

The distinctive boulevard sign is one of four in the 250-home subdivision and is made of heavy timber beams from a former downtown store, Rosenfield's.

The roster of residents, past and present, reads like a who's who of Baton Rouge society. LSU Boyd professors were so prevalent at one time that the saying was, "If you want to be a Boyd professor, you have to live on Nelson Drive."

The home of the late Pulitzer Prize author and historian T. Harry Williams and his wife, Estelle, on Nels Drive was sold to attorney Drew Patty and his wife, Dr. Robin Patton.

Even some historians are unaware that an 1803 plantation home on Menlo Drive was once the Union Plantation home. Originally located at the foot of the Sunshine Bridge, the big house was moved in 1990 by Don Fuson from a site adjacent to Tezcuco Plantation. "Union Plantation was a gift from Marius Bringier to his daughter, Elizabeth, when she married Augustin Tureaud," said Fuson. "It has the original windows, pegged doors, twelve-foot ceilings and Greek Key trim, a sign of wealth then. The tongue-and-groove cypress siding is very rare. When you enter the ten-foot center hall from the gallery, you can see all the way to the back gallery." Fuson and Cecil Patin renovated the home.

A turn-of-the-century house was moved from downtown on Hypolite Street, now North Sixth Street, to Chandler Drive by Dr. and Mrs. Bill Hines. "It was the Sigma Nu Fraternity House when LSU was downtown," said Hines. "When I bought it, it was going to be torn town. Tom Darensbourg, a master carpenter, was in charge of the move."

Few subdivisions have a complete history, but Julia Hawkins and Constance Navratil wrote and published *University Acres & Highland School: A History* in 2004. Many contributed to the in-depth development—complete with maps, plats and photographs of school activities and staff, homes and residents—with remembrances and stories. It is a rich compilation.

A WALK THROUGH WOODSTONE

The first homeowner in Woodstone subdivision, adjacent to University Acres, was Becky Hendry in 1975. She has a picture showing the house that she and her late husband, Gary, built, standing alone in the fields. In 1973, Woodstone was mostly pastureland, a pecan orchard and a small farm.

The main developer, Walter Bankston, said that he started buying the land from the Percy Roberts family in 1961 and finished in 1971. He recalled:

> *I worked with Don Hayden and several others, and they named it Woodstone. We started selling lots at the end of 1973.*
>
> *I wrote the first restrictions in Baton Rouge that mandated a homeowners' association and also mandated that the association has the right to lien property if people do not pay their dues. I did the same thing later when*

I developed Woodgate. I was following the way things were being done in Atlanta. When dues are voluntary, you don't get the level of participation.

The land for Woodstone and Woodgate were jointly owned by Roberts and Harry Nelson, partners who purchased four hundred acres together.

Woodstone has hardy camaraderie, with its homeowners' association headed by Pennie Cotter, a men's walking group and a ladies' book club. It has social events and safety measures for residents. A guardhouse stands at its one entrance-exit on Woodstone Drive.

Pennie said that she and her husband, Greg, would drive around Sundays looking in the area and watched the brick and stucco house being built. When the owners were transferred to Houston, the Cotters bought it even before the owners moved in. They installed a heated swimming pool and bathhouse. The spacious home of 3,400 square feet includes four bedrooms and three baths.

During her tenure as president, Pennie has seen the guardhouse renovated and more illumination provided, entrance signs redone and a glassed-in information sign installed. Also, the entrance sprinkler system was extended and tennis courts were resurfaced. Plans include refurbishing of the clubhouse and renovation of the playground.

"We have great officers and work together," she said. She recalls a great block party and an earlier zoning fight with citizens banding together to stop Boone Drive from being cut through to adjacent Woodgate, keeping intact the one and only entrance to Woodstone.

Once a Civil War Camp: Woodgate

Dr. Ronnie and Louann Bombet bought one of the first homes in Woodgate, the site of a major Union camp during the Civil War. The subdivision off Highland Road has its share of safe cul-de-sac streets, a friendly homeowners' association and many young married couples and children. "When we bought our home in April 1982, there were about eight houses here," said Louann.

The privacy afforded by the one entrance-exit, Woodgate Boulevard, makes for a bonded neighborhood. Developed in 1981 with 230 lots, Woodgate mandates in its restrictions that residents pay dues and belong to the homeowners' association. When Bombet and Peggy Gammill, the daughter of developer Walter Bankston, entertained those first residents at a crawfish boil, the association was launched.

Woodgate had first and second filings with the last thirty lots, Woodgate Estates, in the rear. Early developers included Jim Sumrow and Don Hayden. Bankston was the main developer of both Woodgate and its companion subdivision, Woodstone. The subdivision has a high ratio of professionals, including physicians, LSU faculty and staff and Dow and Exxon employees.

A great number of Woodgate's children attend St. Jude Catholic School. When the bus turns into Woodgate on weekday afternoons, one after another child in uniform gets off to waiting mothers. University Laboratory School is also widely represented.

"I watched my father develop Woodgate," said Peggy Bankston Gammill, wife of Joey Gammill. "We love being close to LSU, baseball and football games." Their three children grew up riding their bicycles to their friends' homes. They also enjoy the three-quarter of an acre lot with a pool and 3,900-square-foot brick home. The long, rear gallery with rocking chairs and a covered outdoor kitchen area, affording a barbecue pit and television,

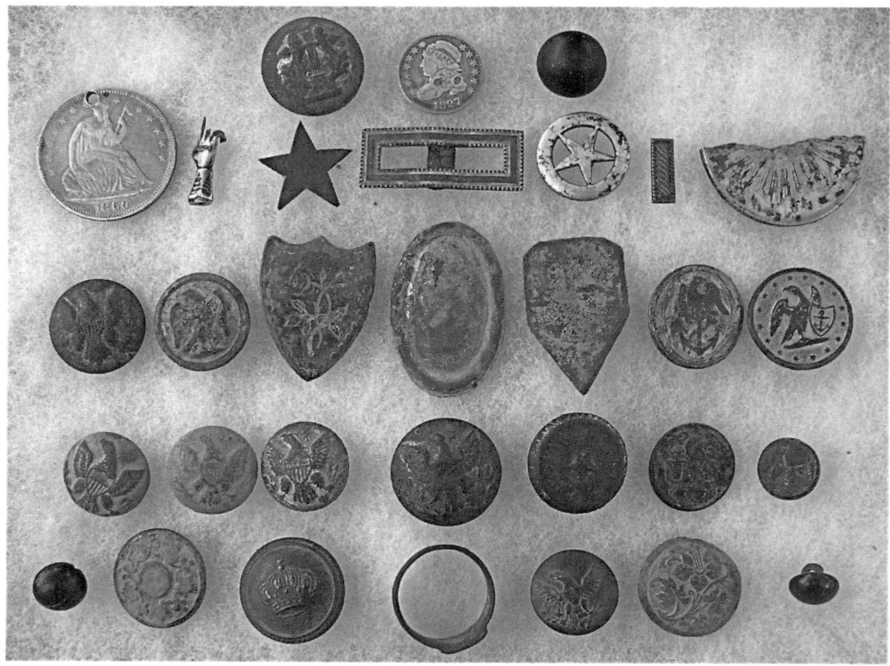

Military artifacts, 1812–64, including Confederate and Union uniform buttons, coins and other Civil War accoutrements, from the Fisher Plantation site, now Woodgate subdivision.

make for year-round entertainment. They also enjoy sitting on benches outside and entertaining neighboring families.

The Bombets needed a larger home and like the floor plan of their 3,200-square-foot home, with its arched courtyard entrance, long back porch and rear lawn.

Drs. Scott and Penny Nelson and four children reside in their second Woodgate home in Millgate Place, which also curves into a cul-de-sac. "We moved from the boulevard to this larger 3,900-square-foot home," Penny said. "We already loved the area. Scott grew up in nearby University Acres." They say that St. Jude is like a neighborhood school.

"This was a new development when we moved here in May 1990," said Doug Williams, attorney and president of the association. He and attorney John Heinrich lead the association, which held a picnic recently. "I like the looks of the area."

As for Woodgate's history, Ward Reilly, a historian, has documented in photographs and text the artifacts he uncovered toward the back portion of the subdivision. "It was the site of a major Federal camp," said Reilly, who got permission to use his metal detector, which uncovered artifacts when the subdivision was under development. "The perimeters of the camp were between South Fieldgate Court and North Fieldgate Court and Woodgate Boulevard," he said. "I first read of the camp in a book by the late Powell Casey, *The Encyclopedia of Forts, Posts, Named Camps and Other Military Installations in Louisiana, 1700–1981*, and assumed it to be Fisher Plantation."

The Relatives in the Central Highland Area

Italian immigrants lived, worked and owned truck farms in the Central Highland Road area in the late 1800s and early to mid-1900s. Many descendants prosper today in this area of 470 homes between Kenilworth and Woodgate subdivisions on Highland Road going back to Bayou Duplantier. The area, with probably more residents who are relatives than any other in the city, is tied together by the Central Highland Civic Association.

Where farmland existed are well-maintained brick homes and awe-inspiring trees. Today at the dead end of Wylie Drive, one mile from Highland Road, is a private club, Mirabeau Gardens, with a swimming pool and tennis courts. Its shareholders are from other areas as well, and all are key holders to the gated facility.

"A bunch of families owned both sides of Highland Road, farming one side and living on the other," said resident Theresa Spedale, the wife of historian-author William Spedale. "My great-grandfather, Cologero Mascarella, was among the families who lived on the Mississippi River side of Highland Road, their property ending at Bayou Fountain, and farmed on this side of Highland."

The Cusimanos, Territos, Mascarellas, Russos and Martinas once farmed this area. "Many of us are related somehow," said Theresa Spedale. "These were plowed fields. When we built our house in 1961, we could still see the furrows."

Genealogist Lucian Mascarella of Baker, who grew up in the area as one of ten children, noted that Cologero Mascarella, his grandfather, purchased seventy-six acres on March 9, 1912, from William E. Fleniken. "These families came from Alia, Sicily, near Palermo in the late 1800s," he said. "They came on boats into New Orleans, where they were taken to sugar cane plantations. The last plantation they worked was Ashland-Belle Helene. I have pictures of the quarter where my family lived. The Mascarella family property went from Highland Road to Bayou Duplantier, in the area that is Highland Park Drive today."

From ages ten to seventeen, he worked on the farm of his father, Charles, and said that when he returned from serving in the U.S. Marines in 1959, he found that the property had been subdivided in 1955–56.

Vincent Russo, retired engineer, still lives on family property on Menlo Drive. He and his wife, Lorena, built their house in 1962 and reared seven children there. "My father, Anthony 'Neno,' bought thirty acres for fifty dollars an acre in the 1930s and sold some in 1959," he said. He has siblings in the area.

Living in his family home on four acres on Highland Road, with a brother still in the farming business, is A.J. Territo, one of seven children. "I was born in this house and have lived here all my life," he said. His parents, children of immigrants from Sicily, built the cypress home in 1930, using some lumber from an older house on the same site they bought in 1912. The rear of the home is on stilts, with windows overlooking the vast, sloping lawn and wooded area.

Today, Mirabeau Gardens is the name given to the major parts of Wylie and Seyburn Drives, off Highland Road. The Territo Tract is in the front of these thoroughfares and on Highland. "It's still the Territo Tract," said Territo, displaying the plats. "This is the way it looked in 1955 when the development started. The land ran from Highland Road to Bayou

Duplantier. My grandparents had fifty acres they purchased in 1912 for fifty dollars an acre, and my father's sister, Nancy Cusimano, had twenty-five acres." At the same time, Cologero Mascarella purchased seventy-six acres, divided among his sons Charles, Anthony and Joe Mascarella. "My family kept six acres, sold in 1955 to become seventeen lots on Highland and the front of Wylie Drive."

Fred Dent Jr. recalled that his parents, Lucille May Grace and Fred Dent Sr., developed seventeen acres in the front part, land bought from the Spaht family.

"Many of the 150 original charter members of the association, formed in 1982, still live here," said Beverly Rodriguez, the first president of the association. Its traditions include three yard awards and a Christmas decoration contest. While the neighborhood clubhouse is a separate entity, with its own officers, it has many families of residents involved. A children's swim team and July 4 party are anticipated annually.

Seclusion and Neighborliness: Highland Bluff Estates

Near the Kenilworth entrance on Highland Road, Ikey and William P. "Bill" Hewes Jr. live in an 1836 white planter's cottage on four acres, bringing a sense of history and warm friendship to the lives of area residents. "Bill and Ikey are like family to Steve and me," said Connie Diniz, who lives on Copperfield Court's west circle that adjoins the Heweses' backyard.

A mainstay in the Highland Bluff Civic Association, Connie said, "We have the best of worlds here. We're near Highland Road but we have the seclusion of a small-town community."

The Dinizes reside in one of the subdivision's thirty-three homes, which vary in style and rest on large lots on Steeplechase Avenue and Copperfield Court. When not working with her husband in their business, Diniz Design Granite Slate and Stone, she could be having tea with Ikey Hewes or rambling around their land, petting their goats, Doc and Gremlin, and their Shetland pony, Frito.

The Hewes family has owned the land and two-story white cypress house at 7541 Highland Road since 1890. Prior owners were various members of the Sharp, Randolph and Kleinpeter families.

Among Hewes's treasured belongings is a board on which these words were written: "This house was built for Miss Adeline Kleinpeter by S.A. Gotham

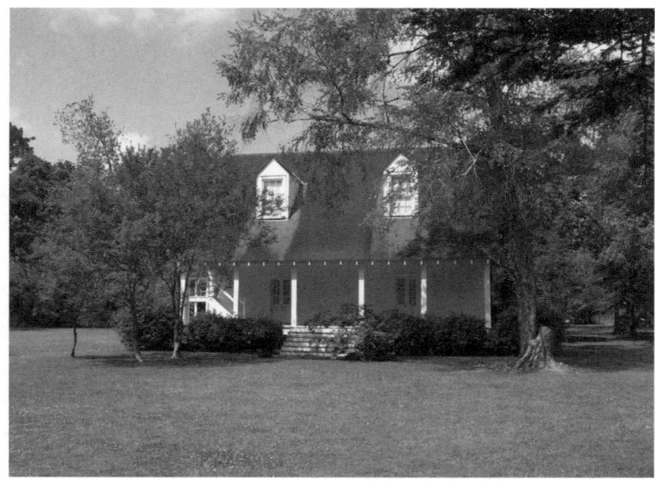

This 1836 planter's cottage near the entrance of Highland Bluff Estates is home to Ikey and William Pilant Hewes Jr., in his family since 1890.

and James Dawson the year 1836." He also has the sale papers from when his grandfather, C.L. Hewes of New Roads, bought the plantation land from Kate Hillman on November 11, 1890, then valued at $2,500 to $3,000. C.L. and Sally Pilant Hewes reared their three children there."

"A year after we were married in 1964 we built a house across Highland Road, where we lived until we moved here," said Bill Hewes. They reared their children, Anna Hoge and Stephen Hewes, here and made extensive renovations. The extensive raised front porch and the four original rooms are intact. Exposed beams and the original colors, turquoise and cream, are in the original cottage section. They built a cottage for Bill's mother in the rear yard, where they have a large garden and enjoy their animals.

Bill said that after he and his siblings inherited the property, they sold more than seventy acres to Steve Wicker and Louis Landry for additional Kenilworth development in 1984. They sold fourteen acres to Rick Hartley, who developed the first part of Highland Bluff Estates. The Heweses developed lots on nearby Menlo Drive in 1989 and added seven lots in Highland Bluff West, located in the west circle of Copperfield Court.

Next door is a plantation-style, two-story brick house built in 1994. Each house, although different, blends naturally into the landscape, even the unique brick and stucco house that Steve Diniz designed in the Frank Lloyd Wright Prairie Years Arts and Crafts style. "We built in the middle of the Heweses' pecan orchard," Connie said. The one-of-a-kind home is a showplace for stone and the Wright style of living, and it includes two original Frank Lloyd Wright chairs and family pieces.

Nature's Neighborhood: Magnolia Woods

Magnolia Wood Avenue, a 1.2-mile thoroughfare that turns off Historic Highland Road, got its name from its developers: Fred G. Benton Jr., Thomas H. "Tommy" Benton and Mary Elizabeth Kenyon, siblings. "The beautiful magnolia trees are the reason for the name," said attorney-preservationist Fred Benton Jr., originally placed in charge of developing the avenue. Other developers were the late Mack Hornbeak and the late W.A. Cooper. The civic association later adopted the name.

"When the late Brice Tomlin and I surveyed the land in 1952, we found a wealth of big trees in a vast variety of species, some probably over one hundred years old," said Fred Benton Jr. "We made a map and inventoried the trees not to be cut close along the mandated fifty-foot right of way, kept as many as possible."

Recalling the difficulties in surveying, he said, "I used dynamite and blew up the stumps to clear the right of way in some places. We used a pull saw to salvage the logs."

Fred had just returned to Baton Rouge after four years in the U.S. Navy in the early 1950s when he undertook the avenue project. He said:

> *Some 120 acres, suitable for three tiers of lots, had been purchased originally by our mother, Emma Cockerham Benton. She was approached by Mack Hornbeak, who owned an adjacent tract of land with W.A. Cooper and wanted the development. We ran a road right down the center and named it Magnolia Wood.*
>
> *Mother sold the land to all three children. The first Magnolia Woods filing was April 1, 1953. We then developed Castle Kirk, first filing on August 15, 1958, with the fourth filing in Magnolia Woods and the second part of Castle Kirk on May 23, 1966, with my younger brother Tommy doing all of the business arrangements.*
>
> *One of the best investments we ever made. I remember that when our mother bought the wooded pastureland nobody else wanted, my father referred to it as "Emma's Folly."*

The first house built was that of Fred Jr. and his wife, Courtney, on the corner of Highland Road at Magnolia Wood Avenue. It has twenty-two acres still undeveloped and a sunken road that could have been the north line of the Union Civil War stockade. Many remain unaware that the Highland Stockade, a Union fortification, existed during the Civil War. It is still visible on the private property of Grant and Tanya Kennedy across Highland.

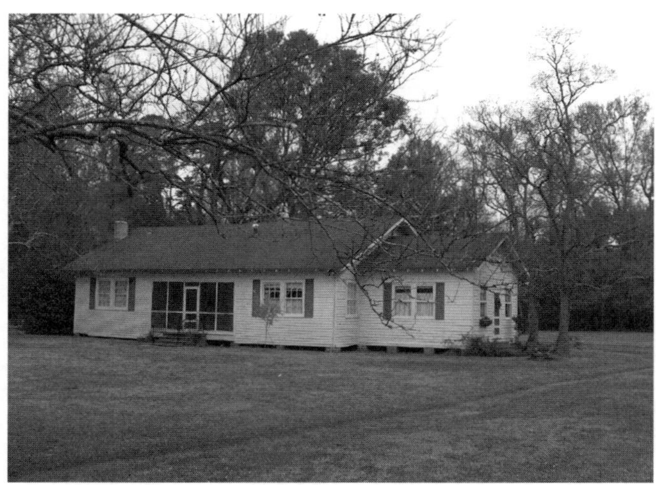

This 1936 farmhouse of Emma and Fred Benton Sr., near Magnolia Woods's entrance, was built on wooded pasture land that her husband called "Emma's Folly."

An aerial photograph shows a "buffalo wallow" that Fred Benton Jr. dug out to become a pond. While surveying, he found buggy axles, a cattle dipping vat and old gray stone U.S. government survey markers. "We tied them in with our survey," he said, noting that he had seen only one other dipping vat, this at Live Oak Plantation Home in West Feliciana Parish.

The development had real obstacles. One harrowing story involved a group of thugs who beat up a construction crew to install a pipe line. Pipeline contractor Jimmy LeBlanc, home from Korea, managed to block the road and put up a fight. "I yelled to Courtney to call the sheriff, and although they finally escaped, they were apprehended and prosecuted. The newspaper ran a story."

The Bentons often greeted adversaries with kindness. When large groups of picketers appeared at the construction site near the family home where Emma Benton resided in an old farmhouse, she served coffee to them. Widowed in 1981, Emma Benton lived here until she died at ninety-two in 1991.

Fred Benton Jr. wrote a book, *Emma*, on his mother's life, including her upbringing at Castle Kirk Plantation near Natchitoches.

Among the first to purchase in Magnolia Woods were Charles and Mary Lollie Garvey, who paid $3,000 for their 131- by 248-foot lot at the entrance of Magnolia Wood Avenue and Highland, across from the Bentons, and built a house of Mohave stone. They bought a third lot and planted live oaks in 1956. "A great place to rear our children," was their consensus, noting the swimming pool and clubhouse for the subdivision that provided summertime fun.

Residents rejoice in the park atmosphere, wildlife and the large lots that generally measure at least 100 by 230 feet. A forceful civic association for 750 homes and volunteer Citizens on Patrol work together.

"Our general area is from Highland Road past Chandler Drive and from Rodney Drive to Kimbro Drive next to Staring Lane. Lynwood Village is also included," said Magnolia Wood Civic Association president Deloris Heagler. "Magnolia Wood Elementary School is in our area." Magnolia Wood Clubhouse and pool, on Magnolia Wood Avenue, has stock and memberships.

The extensive area brings in land developed by Albert H. Hart, as well. William "Butch" Hart recalled that in 1950 his father, the late Albert H. Hart, bought 150 acres on Highland Road back to Dawson Creek, abutting Mount Hope Plantation, then the Hammatt property, and the Rodneys on the other side. "In 1952, Dad took the front 60 acres, put a street down it, Albert Hart Drive, and developed it. He sold lots in Highland Road Estate. My mother, Eleanor Kleinpeter Hart, planted whole acres with St. Augustine grass, day lilies, azaleas and all kind of flowers. Then we moved into our two-story house on a hill. It was country out here."

His father and Sidney Coxe owned Hart-Coxe Construction Company and a lumber company on Highland Road. They built houses across the area, and "Butch" Hart developed Walden subdivision.

The historian Ward Reilly resides on Kimbro Drive but grew up on Magnolia Wood Avenue and has many relatives in the area. His father, the late Bob Reilly, founded the Baton Rouge Civil War Round Table with Fred Benton Jr. "Highland Road was the south entrance to the city during the Civil War," he said and pointed out the breastworks, trenches and even the gun position where the Highland Stockade stood. "This property was also the setting for the original Highland Road School, built in 1910 in the midst of the emplacements, according to Powell Casey's book *Encyclopedia of Forts, Posts, Named Camps and Other Military Installations in Louisiana, 1700-1981*. I assumed this was Fisher Plantation."

The Elegance of the Myrtles

Large tracts of land surround each gracious home in the Myrtles and its pocket subdivision, Myrtle Ridge, a rare circumstance in well-populated South Baton Rouge. Fronted by historic Highland Road with Bluebonnet Swamp to the rear, it combines elegance with privacy. The one entry-exit,

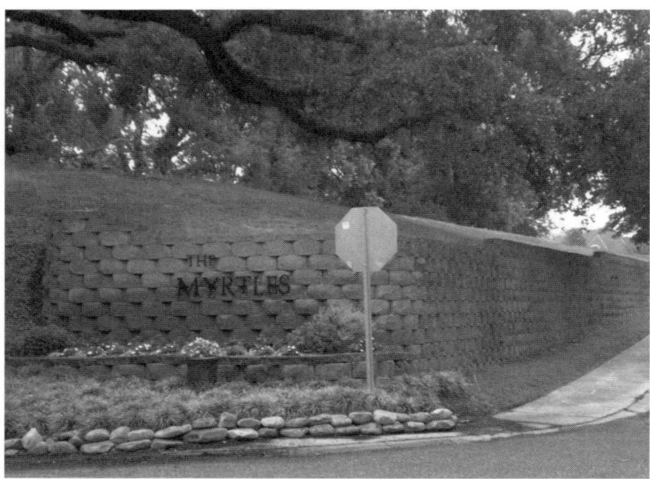

High on a bluff is the Myrtles entrance, built of modular block retaining walls, paid for by the homeowners. *Photo by Kenny Armstrong.*

Myrtle Hill Drive, on a Highland Road bluff off the 9800 block, can be easily missed.

"We love living here," said neurosurgeon Dr. Anthony S. "Tony" Ioppolo, who with his wife, Susan, moved to Baton Rouge in 1978. Native New Yorkers, they have three children and enjoy four acres and a private pond stocked with catfish and bream. Their French chateau–style house is located in a cul-de-sac, Myrtle Hill Drive, with the backyard sloping down to the swamp.

Walter Bankston developed the Myrtles, starting in 1978, after purchasing the acreage from Dr. H. Paulsen Armstrong and his sister, Anna Marie Armstrong Hall. After the Myrtles was developed, Armstrong developed Myrtle Ridge in 1994 and donated some land to the Bluebonnet Nature Conservancy, later sold to BREC.

The first house on Myrtle Hill Drive was built by Dr. and Mrs. Louis Barbato, who moved here for a larger home and lot. "Dr. Bob and Arlene Earhart built right after we did, and it began building up quickly," said Trenny Barbato.

Dr. Bill Hagemann, orthopedic surgeon, is president of the Myrtles Homeowners Association, with thirty homeowners. He and his wife, Mary Rose, purchased 1.7 acres in 1981 and built their home in 1983. "We like the privacy and the birds and wildlife," Hagemann said. The family has lived many places, including five years in Paris, where his mother still lives. She met his father there during World War II, he noted.

In the civic association, Hagemann works closely with Carol Goldsmith and Jess Griffin.

The Goldsmiths enjoy their modified Acadian brick home with a long front gallery, also on Myrtle Hill Drive. They have an herb garden, plus pear, fig and plum trees and blueberry bushes. Carol likes to serve tea with her homegrown mint. She and David are gardeners; she does home canning using their produce.

Another gardener is Mike Bourgeois, who shares fruit and food with the Greater Baton Rouge Food Bank and other charities. He and his wife, Jacqueline, have four generations in their home, including her father, Fred Greer, and a granddaughter, Alexandra. Their two-story brick house rests on one and a quarter acres.

The Ioppolos's palatial home has spectacular views inside and outside and features an interior balcony overlooking a mammoth chandelier and downstairs den. Ioppolo has an array of collectibles, including early American and French clocks, a Napoleon campaign table and armoire once used as a confessional in a French church, antique cars and more. The interior has an Old World look. Several magazines have featured the home and setting.

Living on the swamp, too, are Curtis and Sadie Foshee on Myrtle View Avenue. Their home has a thirteen-foot drop from the wraparound rear gallery overlooking the rear terrain. Nine months of the year they entertain on their back deck, with room for family, including grandchildren.

The homeowners in these adjacent, exclusive subdivisions have pride in their property, as seen in the entrance. More than ten years ago, each homeowner gave $1,000 to build the modular concrete retaining walls, replacing deteriorating railroad ties.

Small but Splendid: Knox Hill

Diminutive and delightful, the thirteen-acre Knox Hill subdivision unfolds prominent names from Louisiana's past and charming one-of-a-kind homes. Located off Highland Road between Gardere Lane and Bluebonnet Boulevard, it was developed by David Vey and Rick Hartley and named for the descendants of Nathan King Knox, who acquired the property in 1877. The land descended through Nathan's brother, James Knox, and his heirs, remaining in the Knox family until 1981, when William C. Knox died.

Along came preservationist-attorney Robert H. Hodges, who purchased the circa 1800 residence known as the "Old Knox House" and, with the subdivision development imminent, moved it to 5544 Highland Road in 1985 and restored it. After tedious research, he renamed it the Joseph Petitpierre House because the original builder obtained a Spanish land grant in 1787 as Joseph Petitpierre, which is French for Kleinpeter. The home has been featured in national and area publications.

A short but sweet ride into Knox Hill includes two streets, each ending in a cul-de-sac, and has one entrance-exit, Knox Hill Drive. Like the Myrtles, it backs up to BREC's Bluebonnet Nature Conservancy. Four families share the swamp view and a large pond, enlarged from an existing small pond; these homes have pie-shaped lots that widen toward the back.

The architectural styles range from a plantation-style rose brick home to an Old English with a dome and courtyard. Each home was tailored for the owners, interior and outside, where garden beauty is the focus. One example is the backyard of Charles and Joanne King, with its four-step stone waterfall sloping down to their swimming pool. Even in the heat of summer, the shady, landscaped properties provide sanctuary.

THE FRENCH FLAVOR OF IBERVILLE TERRACE AND BRIARCLIFF

"The late attorney Joe Gladney knew his French history," said Zeke Dunaway, one of the developers of the first two filings in Iberville Terrace in 1967. "Joe named Iberville Terrace for French explorer Sieur d'Pierre LeMoyne Iberville, who dubbed the capital city Baton Rouge in 1699. Gladney, who held a minor interest, also named the streets." In the third filing, the late Roy LeBouef, a major developer, named Rue Desiree and Rue Clarice for his granddaughters, Desiree and Clarice. On Rue LeBouef Drive is a BREC Park, Rue LeBouef Park.

In this land of bluffs and hills sloping down from Highland Road, Briarcliff and Iberville Terrace are intertwined. Briarcliff off Highland Road, developed by the late Bo Forbes, came first in 1961; it was entered only via a cul-de-sac drive named Huntington Drive, near Oak Hills subdivision. Six years later, Iberville Terrace began development off Highland with a double boulevard entrance on Rue de la Place.

Dunaway developed the first and second filings off Highland Road with the late DeWitt Braud and Charles Bradley, partners who built many of the first homes there. Then, it was all farms and woods. He said that as late as 1941, two sections were known as Ingleside Plantation and Sunny

Bank Plantation, while Abraham and William Adler owned a third section. The second filing brought the double boulevard entrance on Perkins Road, next door to Oakridge subdivision, making a circuitous route that connects Highland and Perkins Roads.

The tranquil lake was easy work, Dunaway said. "It was a natural ravine. We fixed a dam across it so that it would not get any higher than it is now. Later the lake was deeded to the homeowners living on it; most is now fenced by residents, who have made it a private lake."

Today, the well-groomed subdivisions retain their Acadian flair with numerous brick houses with porches and shutters.

Jerry Piper bought his home on Rue Desiree in 1991, later discovering that in 1895, M.A. Piper, his ancestor, owned a large portion of the 311 acres.

Chuck Taylor remembered when his parents, the late Elton and Ruby Taylor, bought a house in the first filing in Briarcliff. Later, in 1967, he bought a house on Huntington Drive across from his parents'. "Briarcliff is real quiet, and we have few problems," said Taylor. "I remember when Highland Road was gravel from Gardere Lane on out and there was nothing but woods. When I was about twenty-one years old, we used to hunt for rabbit and squirrel behind our homes. This was a hog field, where a man used to raise and run hogs."

Octogenarian Isabell Weaver recalled when her husband, the late Earl Weaver, and two daughters kept horses at the nearby Kleinpeter Farm. "We moved here in October 1968, into this brand-new house to be near the horse lot, when the street was not yet completed," she said.

Early residents David and Betty Butler moved onto Rue de la Place on March 1, 1969. "We didn't have a school bus, and I had to take the children to school. This is home, and we have very good neighbors. Thomas and Pat Ranzino moved out here the same time we did." A retired nurse, Patricia Ranzino, likes their Braud-Bradley home.

Early residents included Sam and Phenie Jerome and Russell "Bucky" and Kay Losavio. Kay recalled that she had to take garbage to Highland Road when they first moved there in February 1968.

Association president Dan Cousins noted the good teamwork. "Many contributed to the upkeep in lighting the entranceway, rebuilding signs and erecting a small fence around the waste treatment facility on Rue Desiree. The sheriff's department patrols the area."

Association vice-president Julie Guerin recalled that she and her husband, Todd, bought in 1993 to be near her mother, Lou Fontenot, two doors away.

"It's always been home out here to me. As a kid, I fished and played on the lake, rode my bike and built forts with the other kids." She added that she likes the generational mix of residents, including those who have stayed friends for decades along with new faces moving in.

MAN-MADE LAKES AND STRICT RESTRICTIONS: OAK HILLS

One of the fondest boyhood memories of Russell Kleinpeter Jr. is of riding a cotton wagon down Highland Road from his family farm to a gin at Kleinpeter Station. He and his friends hunted, fished, rode horses and thrived on the country air on property now known as Oak Hills Place and Oak Hills Park. The adjacent subdivisions have ten filings and more than six hundred homes characterized by several man-made lakes.

When first developed, the only entry to both subdivisions was off Highland Road. Today, there is also an entry off Perkins Road into Oak Hills III, another area governed by its own civic association, and a third entry off Siegen Lane.

"When Randall and I moved here, we were in the middle of nowhere," said Margaret Goodwin. "Now we are in the heart of everything." The couple wed in 1949 and were newlyweds when Walter Bankston built their home on the lake, where they reared four children and now have grandchildren. When Oak Hills Place opened up in 1957, Goodwin sold a lot he had bought in another area of town and built here.

Kleinpeter and Bud Finkenaur developed eight of the ten filings, excluding the large original filing that involved a number of developers and one by Rick Hartley. Kleinpeter also built a twelve-acre lake near Kleinpeter Stables at Pastureview Avenue, one of two large lakes in Oak Hills. The first large lake was dug at the time of the original filing.

"My mother, Maud Kleinpeter, named Oak Hills," Kleinpeter said. "At ninety-four, she lives on original Kleinpeter land on the high bluffs of Highland Road."

Kleinpeter served in the U.S. Air Force and recalled that his father had sold land to the original developers. "We had two hundred acres when I came home in 1959, and in 1964, I began farming here, and later on Bud Finkenaur and I started developing in the back part, called Oak Hills Park. We have been developing ever since. Bob Breaux, an engineer, named the streets bearing western and cowboy names near the stable. These include Masterson, Wyatt and Sundance.

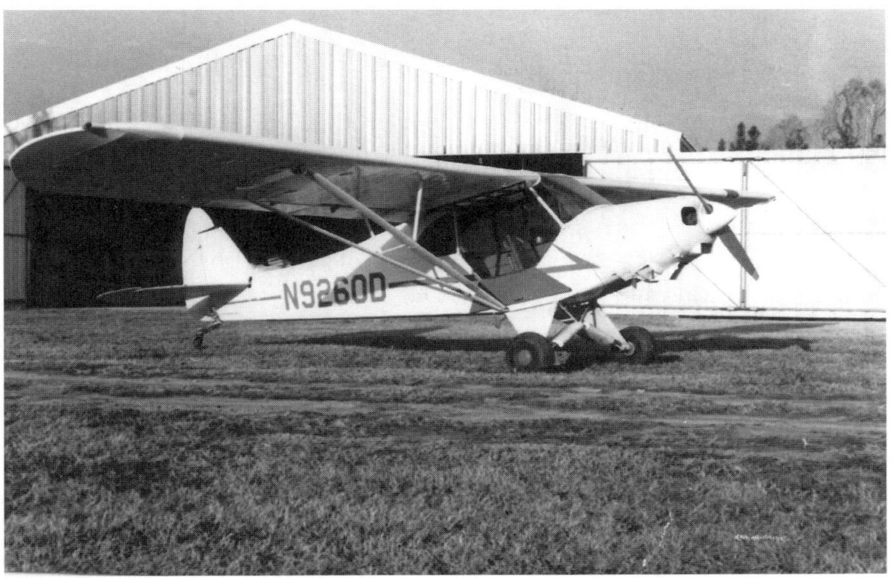

In 1965, Russell Kleinpeter Jr. housed his Piper Cub in a private hangar on what is now Oak Hills subdivision. *Courtesy of Russell Kleinpeter Jr.*

A pilot, Kleinpeter had a private hangar on his property.

Oak Hills Place and Park are in the Greater Oak Hills Civic Association. Within Oak Hills Place, also, is Oak Hills Lake Development Association for homes on the private lake. This group is dedicated to upkeep and cleanliness of the lake, which is well stocked with bass and open only to residents. Lake president is Dr. Michael Puyau, a general surgeon.

The first filing, part one, was developed by four investment groups and signed in the spring of 1957. Its developers included George E. McNutt, Sam G. Dupree, Chester A. McAndrew, Hal S. Phillips and L.W. Collens. Joining the first filing in extended developments were George Paulet and five Barber brothers.

Strict restrictions specified exterior house materials and the number of square feet on the ground and prohibited public buildings, subdividing lots and signs, with the exception of For Sale or For Rent. Also, grass taller than eight inches was mowed and the bill sent to the homeowner.

Hart Investment Company developed the second filing in 1975, also mandating underground electrical distribution.

Third and fourth filings were again companies represented by McAndrew, McNutt, Phillips, Dupree and Airline Terrace Inc., with Barber family members. Rick Hartley developed the fifth filing and Kleinpeter the remaining filings.

Serving her second term as president of the Greater Oak Hills Civic Association, reactivated in the spring of 1997, is Devera Goss. Block captains, a newsletter, area security patrols and great teamwork prevail. Also, a ladies' coffee, wine and cheese gathering and Christmas party are annual events.

As changes came, property values escalated. Also, many original homeowners have children settling in Oak Hills.

Residents thrilled with the location are Richard and Susan Lipsey, who reside on a four-acre peninsula in a beautiful lake. "We were happy seventeen years on eight acres in Iberville Terrace but almost flipped when we saw this location," said Susan. The Lipseys now reside in a luxury home of 6,900 square feet.

Oak Hills III, consisting of 143 homes on three streets, was developed by Walter Bankston in 1978 and has a separate civic association. Its president, Dennis Shaver, assistant track coach at LSU, said, "We like the friendly, well-established and convenient neighborhood."

Classic Southern Plantation Style: Highland Plantation

A sprawling lake and a white wooden fence give Highland Plantation subdivision "the classic Southern plantation feel," in the words of architect Ike Capdevielle, who designed the brick entranceway and fence. "Before the ninety-six-home subdivision was developed by Wayne Heap and Don Hayden, Pati and I decided to move here," said Capdevielle.

Heap said:

> *Don and I started planning it in 1990–91 and began the actual development in 1992. We had been looking for land to develop, and the economy was starting to rally after the slump that began in the mid-1980s. We were able to purchase thirty acres from Gwen Williams. Since the front portion was not good for development, Don and I, along with Ron Ferris of Ferris Engineering and Surveying, decided it would be excellent for a small lake. We landscaped and furnished the lake with water features.*
>
> *Gwen furnished the land for the Highland Plantation Development Group. As we sold lots, she got a percentage of the sales. We had different builders. The lots and houses were sold at such a good clip that we developed*

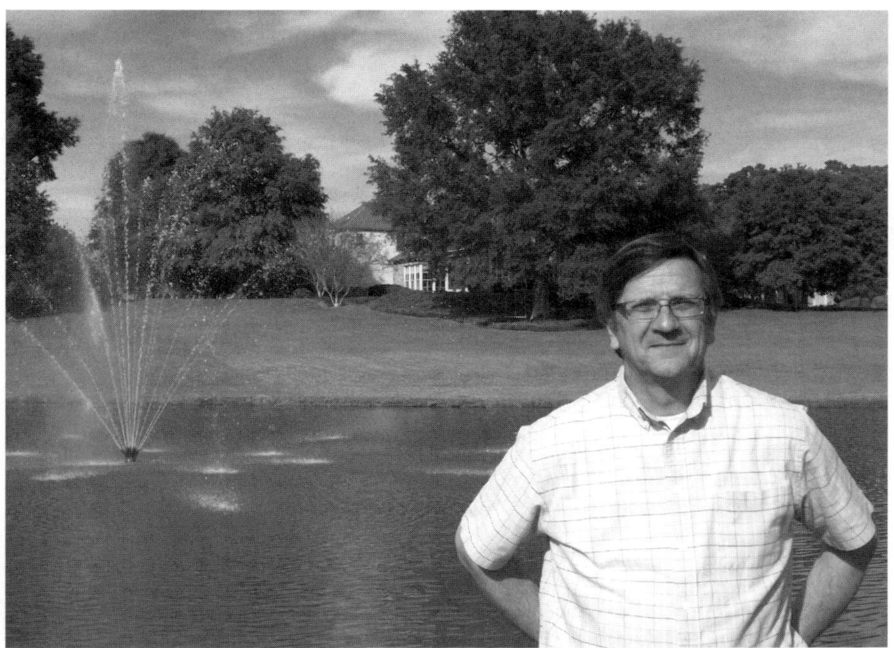

Architect Ike Capdevielle designed and landscaped the Highland Plantation entrance and also the French farmhouse where he and his wife, Pati Bahlinger Capdevielle, reside.

> *second and third filings, simultaneously. Later we bought almost nine acres of adjacent lane from the E. Williams family for a fourth filing, making a total of more than thirty-eight acres.*

The group extended Plantation Ridge Lane, the only entrance-exit, to curve into Plantation Ridge Drive, which became a U-turn leading to Plantation Crest Court. Off the main entry drive are North, South and West Plantation Ridge Courts.

Heap and Hayden, friends, made a good team. They sold lots and built the first home as an example, ending up building one-fourth of the subdivision's homes.

Peter Nyburg, president of the Highland Plantation Property Owners Association, said that he and his wife, Kay, reside on Plantation Ridge Drive in their second subdivision home, opting for a larger home. Their 3,250-square-foot house was built by Wayne Badineaux in 1996. Memorabilia from world travels and military service, including the Purple Heart, adorn the home. Nyberg is a decorated lieutenant colonel, retired, U.S. Army Reserve, and

Kay, also retired, was director of nursing at Baton Rouge General Medical Center and St. James Place health services.

Custom-style houses include that of the Capdevielles, which Ike designed. The two-story French farmhouse was inspired by a trip to Europe and is made for casual living and comfort. Thick native flora and foliage, evidence of Pati's love of gardening, lend to the country aura. A gated office building is in the rear.

Capdevielle served on the association's architectural control committee and was in charge of landscaping the front entry. "We like the fact that the neighborhood is built out and cannot be expanded," Ike said. "We know everybody on our street."

Association dues, mandated in the restrictions, help maintain the common areas, buy and maintain flags and distribute information packets to new residents. A security patrol and socials are part of the activities.

ROLLING HILLS, LAKES AND INDIAN MOUNDS: COUNTRY CLUB OF LOUISIANA

One week before Katrina struck in 2005, John and Nancy Taylor Miller drove through the gates of the Country Club of Louisiana (CCLA) to their new residence, greeted by tranquility, beauty, security and the good feeling of coming home. "Neighbors came over with food and flowers," said Nancy Miller. "Some even brought their children to introduce." The neighborliness intensified in days to come.

Some were unaware that John Miller was the entrepreneur and visionary who had produced their neighborhood, established in 1985. As the initial joint-venture partner with Jack Nicklaus Development Company, Miller obtained the original options on the property, located off South Highland Road near I-10. The Millers and their three daughters had lived in CCLA from 1988 to 1992, then lived in Memphis for twelve years before returning to celebrate CCLA's twentieth anniversary.

When Miller started working on the development in 1983, he was twenty-eight and one of America's first certified financial planners. Having seen world-class developments in other cities, he thought Baton Rouge should have one. As he and attorney Greg Pletsch scrambled to meet option deadlines, he sold the mindboggling idea to thirty-five local founders and raised $14 million in forty-five days.

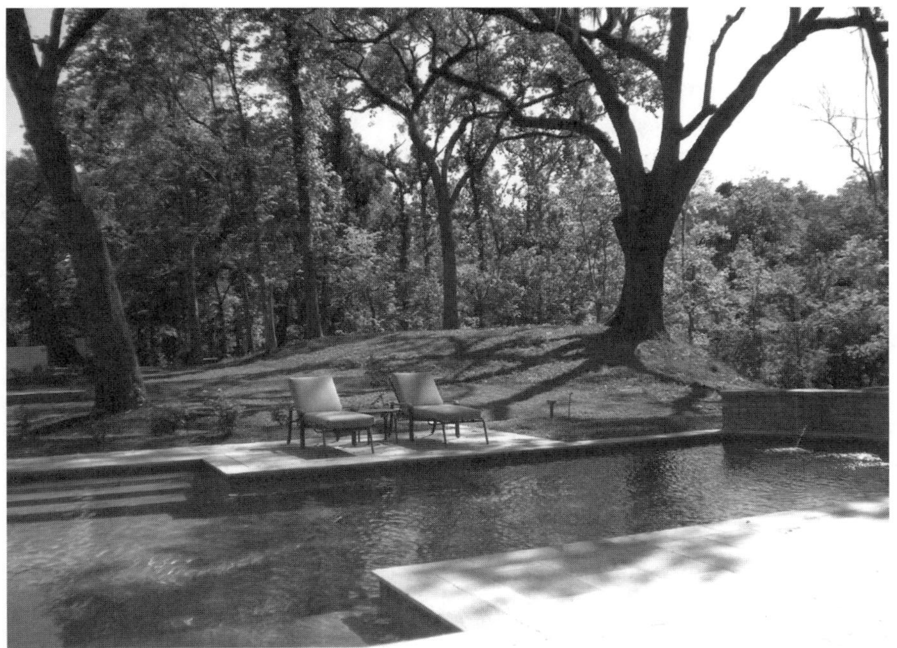

Tony and Rene Graphia have three Indian mounds on their Country Club of Louisiana property, including one near the pool. *Photo by Kenny Armstrong.*

Key to the project were the Moore family, the source of the initial 510 acres; banker Chuck McCoy; and real estate broker Charlie Cole. And in April 1986, at the clubhouse's grand opening, Jack Nicklaus played the course he designed.

Today, there are six-hundred-plus homeowners, six Indian mounds, venerable trees on 844 acres of gently rolling hills and nine lakes. The Kleinpeter Archaeological Site is located at the confluence of Bayou Fountain and Bayou Manchac, visited by French explorer Pierre le Moyne, Sieur d'Iberville, during a journey recorded in his journal of 1699. LSU archaeologists Malcolm Shuman and D.C. Jones were in charge of the mounds' mapping survey and then the excavation. Shuman is impressed by the area's continuity of settlement across the years and is grateful to landowner Alton Moore for allowing access to the country club, as well as to donors. These include the Baton Rouge Area Foundation, Ben Kleinpeter and David and Rose Hunter of CCLA.

This "city within a city," with its abundant wildlife, bayous and lakes, has its own streets, drainage system and streetlights. Here are the amenities of city life with the allure of nature, such as the occasional sighting of a fox running down the golf course.

Streets were named for famous golf courses. The park—with a children's play area, tennis, basketball, volleyball, baseball, soccer and a jogging trail—is the site for socials, including a Halloween party and Christmas tree lighting with a bonfire.

Residents who also belong to the club have the pleasure of gracious dining, swimming, tennis and golfing. The two-story plantation-style clubhouse requires dues, with monthly memberships in golf and tennis/ swim categories.

Leanne Smith, administrator of the Property Owners Association, said that all residents are mandated to pay POA dues. "We build community, offer services and promote social events," she said. A security staff mans the gates controlling access to CCLA and patrols the private streets. Maintenance workers landscape and maintain common areas, including the park and lakes. The club and golf course have their own maintenance employees.

Eight trees are registered with the Louisiana Live Oak Society, verifying that they are at least one hundred years old. Tereasa Olinde, president of the Garden Club, said their members donate trees every year and, after hurricane destruction, also gave $500 to the golf course.

A board of directors is led by Lynn Juban, president, and Norman Chenevert, vice-president. An architectural review panel, one of six POA committees, has strict guidelines; allowed designs include Plantation, Acadian West Indies and French Quarter.

"We have great artists here," said Smith, pointing out a wall that features tiles of animals indigenous to the area. Resident artist Dani Shobe made tiles as a fundraiser for a children's spray park.

In 2005, $100,000 was raised for a community recreation center.

Ted and Penny Hoz poured the first slab in late 1985. "In mid-July we moved in," said Penny. "Two other families were already living here: Ed and Carole Sexton and Bubba and Frances Henry."

Since Thanksgiving 1993, Jerry and Roger del Rio have lived here. Jerry, a real estate broker, is past president of the board of directors; her late father, Charles Sylvest, was one of thirty-five founders. She remembers when a garden home could be purchased for about $250,000. "Now you are hard pressed to find one less than $400,000, and some exceed $2 million," she said.

Connecting Perkins and Highland Roads

Toward LSU

Stanford Place a Standout in Shadows of LSU

Stanford Place was once Jolly's Pasture, and at least one resident, Winkie Rector, would have preferred that name for the subdivision. "More unique," she said.

Henry William "Bill" Jolly III remembered when his parents, the junior Jollys, owned the property. "The whole of Stanford Place was our backyard," he said, recalling when he and his siblings fished, rode horses and rode their bikes to Southdowns School. "My father never wanted the subdivision named for him," said Jolly, who resided with his wife, Margaret, and daughter, Elizabeth Rose, in a house near the entrance on Stanford Avenue. "When developers came over, my brother allowed them to name a street Jolly Drive."

About his home, he said, "My grandparents lived here first, but then they moved their house back and my parents had this house built."

Before the subdivision was developed, a large one-acre pond stood at the entrance. "It was between our house and the house next door, where my aunt Elizabeth Bacot lived. She was my sixth-grade teacher at Southdowns, which was a great neighborhood school." He also attended nearby St. Aloysius Catholic Church.

> *My grandfather also owned cows, ran a dairy out here and developed real estate. My grandmother was Etta Blouin Jolly. This property is still called the Etta Blouin Tract. In the 1848 plantation map, the tract was two thousand acres extending from here to Zeeland Avenue.*
>
> *I remember Grandfather digging out the swamp and piling dirt on the side to make lots to sell. This was before the Civilian Conservation Corps* [CCC] *came out here. He died in 1956, when I was just starting elementary school.*

Developer George E. McNutt Jr. remembered the lake. "We thought it would be neat to have the entrance go around the pond, but the city-parish told us the pond had to go." The developers with him were Rolfe McCollister, Clifford Ourso, Wally Wells and Carl Baldridge.

The children of Rolfe and Dot McCollister grew up in two homes in Stanford Place, one a beautiful large lot overlooking the swamp at the rear, where Dr. Michael and Jeannette Rolfsen and family now reside.

David Hatcher and his family had their home on Floyd Drive built in 1967. "We have great neighbors who look out for each other," he said. "Our security patrol is under the Southside Civic Association. Basically, Stanford Place takes in South Lakeshore Drive, Ross Avenue, Floyd Drive leading to Stephens one way and to Jolly Drive the other, also South Cloverdale."

The first home dwellers were Walter and Hilda Krousel on South Lakeshore Drive. Hilda said:

> *The streets had been laid out and we had sidewalks, but there were just a few spec houses going up when we moved here in 1963. There were horses at the subdivision entrance.*
>
> *I'll never forget when we moved here. I came out one day to line the kitchen cabinets with paper. We wanted to move in before Thanksgiving. We had someone staying with our four kids at our home on Ormandy Drive. Not being used to the quiet, I had the radio on. I hadn't been listening ten minutes when the news came. It still gives me goose bumps. I can show you exactly where I was standing when I heard that John F. Kennedy had been shot on November 22, 1963.*

The Krousels wanted to be close to LSU, where Hilda had a part-time job doing research and earned her PhD in history in 1970. Walter is an attorney.

Commodious homes and large lots are trademarks here. The John Crabtrees and Boyd McMullans are among families who have long enjoyed their South Lakeshore Drive homes.

College Town in LSU's Backyard

Those entering College Town from Highland Road see two large concrete tigers and an attractive wooden sign that spell out a neighborly welcome to the "small town within the city," as described in the subdivision's history. Streets are named for universities, and street names are set in old blue tile into sidewalks.

Developed in 1923, the subdivision is fortunate to have a written history. Each resident has received a booklet with text by Bill and Pat Cooper, longtime residents on Amherst Avenue, and sketches by Una Wilkinson of some of the oldest homes. The late LSU professor Dr. Harold Barr was historical consultant.

"We have 150 homes and are bounded on one side by West Lakeshore Drive and on the other by Highland Road," said Steve Brown, president of the civic association. "Amherst is our westernmost street, and Stanford Avenue near Baton Rouge Beach our easternmost street. Our lots run up to University Lake."

Like University Hills, College Town was created from the farmland of the Denis Daigre family. On June 15, 1923, Pelican Realty Company, owned by the late Berlin Perkins, purchased an undeveloped tract of land. "My father owned Pelican Realty and Pelican Savings and Loan," said Verdie Reece Perkins, realtor. "He developed College Town, put in streets, sidewalks and utilities."

Admiring of his late father, Perkins recalled that the day he entered LSU in 1930, his father lost their home in downtown Baton Rogue. Refusing to declare bankruptcy, B.E. Perkins offered lots in College Town to those whom he owed money but could not pay. The booklet recounts the low price of some lots during this Depression era and compares it to the current value. The price of an average lot in College Town has grown from $7,000 in 1963 to $20,000 in 1973 to well over $60,000 now.

Since nearby LSU made its official move from downtown to the "new" campus in 1925, many faculty and staff lived in College Town. This remains true today.

One of College Town's amenities is University Lake, begun in 1933 and completed in early 1937 as a New Deal program with WPA workers. The booklet describes the men, up to one thousand at a time, cutting down trees in the swamp in this 280-acre extension of City Park Lake.

The city's oldest cemetery, Old Highland, or the Penny Graveyard, is located on Parker Street across from the John M. Agricultural Center. It dates from the 1840s, when Robert and Matilda Penny owned the surrounding plantation. Four Penny children are buried here, along with Armand Duplantier, Pierre Joseph Favrot and other members of pioneer families. Dr. and Mrs. James A. Thom III spearheaded the restoration of the cemetery.

"My family built this house in 1933," said septuagenarian Ruth Lamont, who grew up in her home on LSU Avenue. "My husband Neil and I bought the house from the estate in 1964, did interior changes but the outside is still the same dimensions and solid cypress clapboard." In 1976, the house got a Louisiana Landmarks Plaque. "There is real history in our area. Across the street is a little white house built by Castro Carazo, whom Huey Long hired from the Roosevelt Hotel's Blue room in New Orleans to be LSU bandmaster."

Another longtime resident, Louise Morris, has lived more than fifty years in her Stanford Avenue home and remembered when her one-and-a-half-story brick house was built. She and W.D. Morris, LSU professor, were wed fifty-one years when he died in 1978. "In those days you did not want to owe any money, so we built it on two lots for about $15,000 without borrowing." Morris drew plans for houses and during summer months had them built

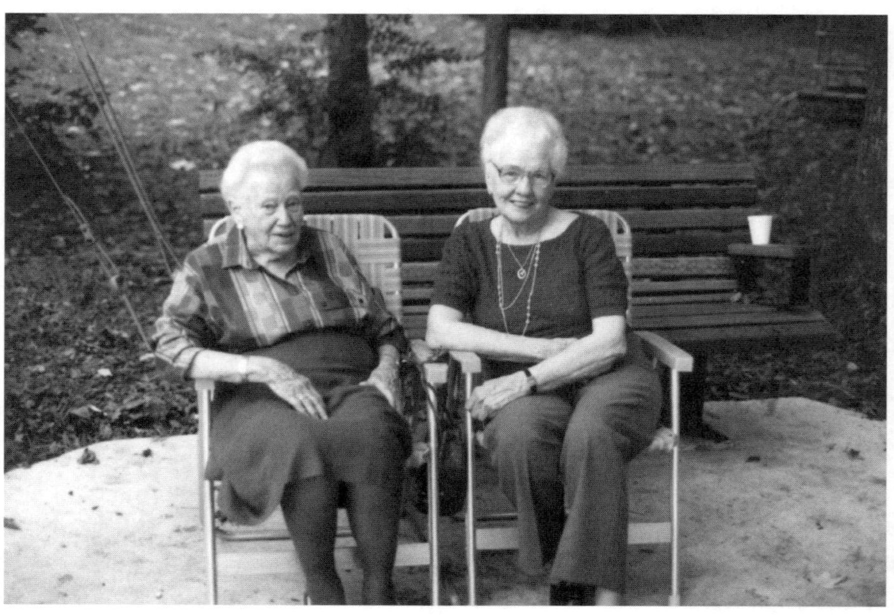

College Town friends Gertrude Wilbert, *left*, and Louise Morris share a neighborhood park bench that Wilbert donated to honor Morris, late 1980s. *Photo by Cynthia Morris.*

and sold them. She recalled when their home was the only one on the west side of Stanford and that of Gertrude Wilbert the only one on the east. The neighbors were friends, and Wilbert gave four benches in College Town Park in Morris's honor.

Next door resides her son, Richard, and his wife, Cynthia, whose garden was on a recent Hilltop tour. Other College Town gardens on past Hilltop tours include June Tuma, Barbara Reilley, Moe and Babs Athmann, E.O. and Mary Timmons, David and Beth Morgan and Lamont.

On Harvard Avenue near the park, septuagenarian Mary Landry Fousse, widow of Joseph Fousse, said it took her husband five years to build their English Tudor home himself. "We call it the House of Seven Gables," she said. The Fousses moved into their home in 1946. They and their small children lived in the garage, converted into an apartment, while it was being built.

The civic association was born in 1973 when a large apartment complex was proposed for the northern edge of College Town. Residents stopped this effort and also kept a restaurant from being built at the entrance, according to Helen Loos, an early organizer, along with George and Lillie Gallagher, Ron Pohl, Lela Schroeder, the late Dr. Harold Barr and Gertrude Wilbert.

The amazing diversity manages to keep the community look, one that Barbara Reilley described as being so much like her native New Orleans near Tulane and Loyola, where she and her husband Ford were reared, that it felt like homecoming when they moved there in 1975.

College Town has brought in two small developments: the homes on West Lakeshore Drive around the lake leading to Parker and Le Havre, an upscale development of twenty-two town homes.

LeHavre and Its Vieux Carre Flavor

LeHavre, which is French for "haven," was part of the historic 1923 College Town tract and remains a private, secluded haven just blocks from LSU. It wasn't until 1978 that Keith Lanneau developed the lakefront town house community with a Vieux Carre flavor and individualized homes. Lanneau, president of East Parker Properties, and his late wife, Joy, pioneered this type of small planned unit development and also wrote the strict subdivision restrictions.

LeHavre may be entered on either Rue Toulouse or Rue Sorbonne off East Parker Avenue, across from the John M. Parker Agriculture Center of the university. "These streets were named for two of the oldest universities in the world," said Lanneau, "in keeping with College Town, where streets are named for American colleges and universities." In developing LeHavre, Lanneau and engineers Clary and Associates faced some major challenges.

"Originally, the property needed filling and was overgrown with large trees, weeds and shrubs," Lanneau said. "I paid to have East Parker paved." He recalled a dirt road known as Lovers Lane that went from the south gates of LSU on Highland Road to College Lake.

Lanneau built six to eight town houses before the economy slumped. "I just held onto lots. At the end of the 1980s, when the new building boom started, I sold them off." With help and advice from various members of the Planning Commission, including the late Don Lynch, the two key streets were closed to through traffic.

Of the twenty-five houses on nearly three and a half acres, three are on College Lake across from West Lakeshore Drive. To the rear is the BREC College Town Park on Oxford Street. In one corner is the Old Highland (Penny) Cemetery, also on Oxford.

The first house, built in 1981, was for Helen M. "Tillie" Cookston, who retired from LSU in 1988 as director of student teachers in the College of Education. Her nephew, W.C. Cookston III of Monroe, was the architect. The two-story house has a courtyard, dormer windows and, a rear patio with a fountain. The stained and etched glass, along with stenciling, are the work of Cookston's niece, Monroe artist Ann Cookston Brown.

Luxury homes include those of David and Beverly Robinson and Bert and Sue Turner, both overlooking the lake. Beverly knew she wanted architect Mike Waller, who calls the home an American town house circa 1830. It has a New Orleans courtyard and porte cochere entered through a two-hundred-year-old wrought-iron gate from Barcelona. "The gate can be locked and is actually the front door to her home," he said. Beverly loves hydrangea, so not only are hydrangeas in her courtyard but also a wallpaper feature in one bath.

The only house on two lots is that of the Turners, whose lakefront, four-level home, often called a chateau, features a French farmhouse design with a tower. Built by Larry Norman with architect Bill Hughes, the house has a gated courtyard entry that lends a homey welcoming aura. "Provence [France] is a favorite place," said Sue. "I looked at a lot of books to get the look we liked." From their master bedroom balcony is a view of the lake and part of LSU. "I can see the sunrise from my bed," she said.

Kenilworth Parkway

A Glowing Neighborhood: Kenilworth

The annual Independence Day Parade and Christmas luminaries make Kenilworth a place of community-wide traditions that draw hundreds of sightseers. Kenilworth subdivision is a spirited neighborhood of some 785 households. Entrances are off Highland Road and Perkins. Walkers enjoy the two-mile trek along the Kenilworth Parkway, entrance to entrance.

The parade features floats and bands. A slow stream of automobiles wends through Kenilworth for the luminaries, usually slated the Sunday before Christmas at 6:00 p.m. Both events have contests for homeowners. Halloween food collections and carol singing to shut-ins at Christmas, plus Resident of the Year, are among other traditions.

Steve Wicker was the developer in 1967, prior to Walden's existence. He said:

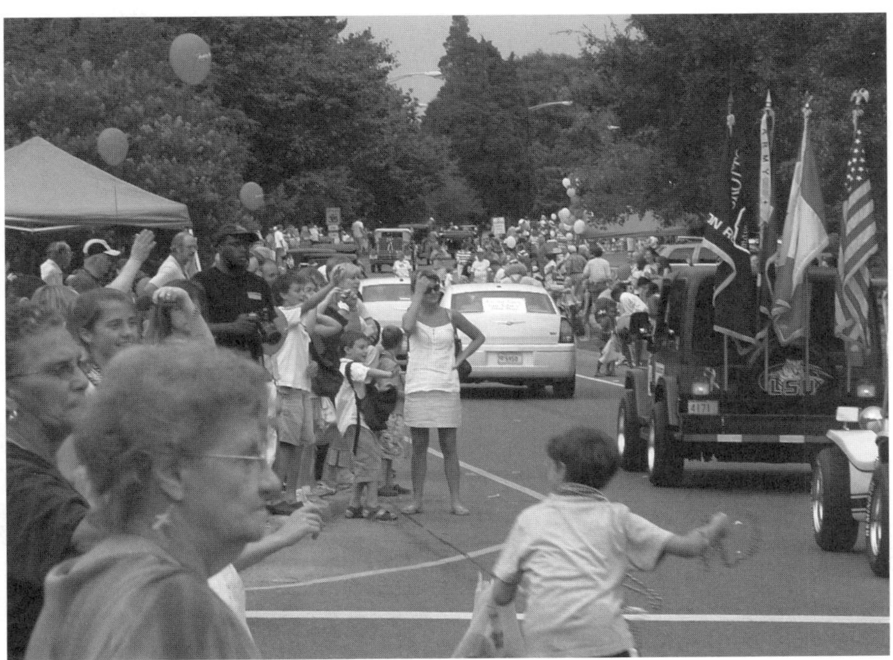

Kenilworth's Fourth of July Parade, a family-style community-wide event, draws thousands of spectators. *Photo by Bob Mathews.*

> *I had a map and book on Kenilworth, England, and named the streets after the English. Architect Richard Caldwell designed the brick structures at the intersection of the Parkway and Menlo Drive that resemble castles with turrets. We planned to construct high-end town houses between Highland Road and the entrance gate, but the recession came in the early 1970s.*
>
> *Kenilworth Inc. originally owned 240 acres, which we had purchased from six or seven families, but we had to sell out to Royal American Corp.*

Cliff Chenier, a resident and contractor, built 250 to 300 homes in Kenilworth over a twenty-eight-year period. He said that when Wicker brought him into the neighborhood, there were two houses on the Parkway and it was open fields.

> *I put up three spec houses, and Gulf States Utilities had a Parade of Homes. At that time Kenilworth was not open all the way to Perkins, and Kenilworth Parkway was the only street here. I built at least sixteen houses on the Parkway.*
>
> *Steve Wicker approached me again when Kenilworth Middle School opened and he was developing Bromley, Daventry, Coventry, Boone and quite a few other streets. He was running short of money, so I bought seventy lots, built the houses and sold them. When Chippenham opened up, I bought ten lots there between Boone and Menlo, all they would give me.*

A World War II veteran who served in the Philippine Islands and engaged in eight landings against the Japanese, Chenier recently completed an addition to the home of his daughter, Virginia Case, on Louray Drive, doing most of the construction work himself. Other major builders in Kenilworth, he said, included Wally Wells, Paul Lemoine, Bradley and Braud.

Retired Gulf States Utilities ad representative Walt Wright helped stage the Parade of Homes and resides with his wife, Carolyn, on Bromley Drive in a Chenier-built home. A Korean veteran in the Air Force, Wright said they moved onto Bromley in 1971. He has served on the board, and Carolyn has served in the ladies' club.

Kenilworth Civic Association (KCA) president Linda Fredericks and her husband, Rodney, bought their home on Chippenham Drive in 1984 and last year remodeled, adding a suite for her parents, Theresa and Bill Gex.

The first formal meeting of KCA took place in February 1972. "We're well set up," said Fredericks, "and no one person has to do too much. We have one of the best directories I have ever seen."

Jack Conran recalled that he was the first "railroaded" KCA president. ("About eight residents got together to organize a nonprofit civic association and dubbed me president.") He and his wife, Marlene, said their house, built in 1971, was one of the first on Bromley, near Highland Road with pecan orchards and fields, some with cattle grazing. "The Parkway stopped in our driveway. We used to chase cows and bulls from our yard," said Marlene.

A separate entity is the Kenilworth Club, situated on eight acres in the vicinity off the Parkway, with a clubhouse, tennis courts and swimming pool. Jerald Juneau, a corporation founder, said that there is a waiting list to buy shares. Laughingly, he remembered his wife Betsy waking him up in the middle of the night when the pool was first built and cold weather came. "I would run to the pool to drain the pipes. I'm glad I don't have to do that anymore."

A Vision Realized: Walden

The poetic philosophy of famed Henry David Thoreau was distributed in literature when Walden was created. A group of design professionals worked together to build the ninety-one and a half acres, with two-thirds of it green area, since the drainage required more than an engineer.

"Butch Hart was way ahead of his time when he put Walden together," said Frank Kean III, a ten-year resident. "Sometimes, en route to work along Walden Road, I have to stop my car and just look at it. When the sun is coming up and I look across the lake to see light through the cypress trees shining off the water, it is so beautiful that it is almost eerie. Walden is a nugget of gold in the city—like being up in St. Francisville."

Residents love the aura of a retreat and cherish the quietude, sounds and scurrying of birds and wildlife and the preservation of trees and plants, including moss-hung cypress trees in two man-made lakes, Walden Pond and Canoe Bend Lake.

Unlike neighborhoods where trees are bulldozed and houses built with no regard for how they fit into the landscape, Walden became the first land in the city developed as a unique cluster community and remains the largest. Houses are clustered with cul-de-sacs for guest parking, small lawns in general and a huge common area that makes residential accessibility to the park setting.

Realtor William "Butch" Hart said his father, Albert H. Hart, bought 150 acres adjacent to Mount Hope Plantation on Highland Road. In 1952, he developed 70 of the acres on Albert Hart Drive and sold lots. In 1956, he built a family home at the end of Albert Hart Drive, moving there in 1957. "I started working part time with Dad when I was in high school and LSU and went full time in 1962. Sam Dupree, the civil engineer in Dad's subdivisions, gave me a book published by Urban Land Institute on cluster development, a new concept then."

A six-member team, six consultants and an architectural control committee worked together. After the senior Hart died on May 2, 1977, Butch Hart built a house on Applewood Drive, on which the majority of Walden homes were built. In 1987, he bought the family home, then on Albert Hart Drive, from three out-of-town siblings. On sixteen acres, it is now included in the Pond, a later development.

Thoreau, who took rare delight in life and the outdoors, wrote, "It is something to be able to paint a particular picture, only to carve a statue, and so to make a few objects beautiful; but it is far more glorious to care and paint the same atmosphere and medium through which we look." Residents have a sense of untrammeled beauty when they look at pictures of Walden Pond that Thoreau enjoyed, similar to their own scenery.

Bo and Ruth Bolourchi, who reside in one of the first five houses built in Walden in 1975–76, have fed the ducks for more than twenty years. "We put some thirty wood duck chalets on the trees where they can nest," said Bolourchi, civil engineer who heads a committee to oversee the quality of water in the lakes and several times president of the homeowners' association. "The wild wood ducks come in around sunrise and sunset, and we have mallards, too," he said. "Residents who fish throw the fish back."

Their two-story brick and wooden home has a deck of 2,850 square feet of air-conditioned area. Ruth likes the floor plan with a sunken den and set-in windows. "When we look out from upstairs, we feel like we're on a houseboat." They have a canoe and ride in the evening. "Living here," said Bo, "is almost like living in a resort without the upkeep of a resort."

A pedestrian bridge over Canoe Bend Lake allows residents to walk across to the other side without driving around.

James S. Vilas, homeowners' association president and realtor, said there is a waiting list. He and his family live on Applewood, only four houses away from his father and stepmother. He said the grounds committee is the toughest, being responsible for the huge common ground. Association fees are adjusted according to the acreage owned.

Community activists Roger and Marcia Moser, along with former LSU basketball coach Dale Brown, are among prominent residents. Many nationalities, a diverse group of professionals, live here.

The clubhouse on Thoreau has a swimming pool and tennis courts. Across Thoreau are attorney Van and Lorri Mayhall. They like their stucco French-style house, completely walled, with a courthouse and fountain in front. "I really enjoy the hills and valleys of this area, which has lots of different features, topography like the East Coast," said Mayhall. "It is not totally flat."

Staring Lane

Lynnewood Village and Ranch-Style Homes

Richard McDowell, realtor, bought the land and started developing Lynnewood Village off Staring Lane in 1955. His attorney, Jack Laycock, persuaded Buck Barber of Barber Brothers Contracting Company to put up the money for him, he said. "Every time I sold a lot, I gave Barber Brothers money for the purchase. I liked the name Lynnewood, and at first called it Lynnewood Park and then changed it to Village."

He named Sharynwood and Laurynwood Drives for his daughters. He and his wife, Thelma, also have a son, Richard "Rick" McDowell Jr., contractor, for whom he named Rickwood and Rickshire Drives in South Hills Division, developed in 1961. Lynnewood Village also brings in some of Kimbro and Chandler Drives.

Two wooden signs on Staring Lane signal entry to the fifty-five lots, averaging 100 by 127 feet, in this place of tall trees and numerous ranch-style houses. Older residents recalled when Essen Lane was a country road flanked by ditches.

"We have the second or third house built here," said Betty Denham, married to Claude Denham, on Chandler Drive. "Before this, we lived in a canal area that flooded, and we wanted this higher site." A flower gardener, once a week she delivered her homegrown bouquets to people and charitable places.

Fred and Bea Van Noy bought their house on Sharynwood Drive on a small hill in 1958 and later expanded it to add a game room, sun porch and shop. In 1971, the oldest of their three daughters, Diana, and her husband, Jim Corbin, moved across the street from them. The Corbins said that every lot had been built on when they moved there and Chandler Drive dead-ended; now Chandler cuts back to Maxine and Baird Streets.

Numerous residents are LSU professionals and like the proximity to the campus. This included Betty Laborde on Kimbro Drive at the corner of Chandler Drive. "It was country when we moved here," she said. "The subdivision was about half full. Now I know some who have lived here thirty years or more." She once served as vice-president of their civic association.

Robert and Brenda Baumann on Kimbro Drive, who have LSU ties, saw their sons, Kyle and Frank, grow up here. "We liked the Magnolia Wood Pool Club," said Baumann. "Lynnewood Village residents could join—a real neighborhood thing and great for the kids in the summer."

Laurel Lea, "Green Meadow"

Alton Leander Lea, a former postmaster and realtor, wanted to buy five acres where his small children could someday ride horses and ended up with a subdivision, Laurel Lea. At age ninety-one, in 2001, Lea said that he had not planned to develop a subdivision and asked John Whitty if he could buy five acres.

"Mr. Whitty said he would sell me the whole tract, 60.79 acres, if he and his wife, Sadie Kimbro Whitty, could keep 1 acre for their home," Lea recalled. He agreed and had plans drawn selecting the name, Laurel Lea. "It's an English term for green meadow," he said.

The trees remain an attraction in this old, established neighborhood of ninety-six lots, developed in 1953–54, that includes that part of Staring Lane starting at Highland Road and extends down the north side of Staring to five lots past Boone Drive. It also brings in Kimbro Drive near Highland Road until it dead-ends at the five acres of Dr. Arthur Moles on Kimbro Drive. Kimbro can be entered off Staring Lane on two cross streets, Menlo and Boone Drives, or immediately behind Laurel Lea Shopping Center. On the other side of Moles's property, Kimbro Drive picks up in Lynnewood subdivision, also off Staring Lane.

Until he had a stroke, Lea served as assistant superintendent of Sunday school and often was a deacon at First Baptist Church downtown. "Our church started Laurel Lea Baptist Church on Staring Lane as a mission," he said. "I donated one lot for the church, and the church added to it. It is now an established church." Later, the church changed its name to New Life of Baton Rouge Church.

Almost the same time that Laurel Lea was developed, Magnolia Woods got underway. The residents of Laurel Lea are included in Magnolia Woods Civic Association. Early residents watched much of Magnolia Woods subdivision being built.

Moles, a retired dentist, got his love of the outdoors naturally, since his father, Hunter S. Moles, was a horticulturist with LSU. At age seventy-seven, in 2001, he said he cut his own lawn with a tractor and loved gardening. He had his house designed to go with the woods. "I can look out the windows and see in every direction. It's very private here, and the trees and shrubs are beautiful. We have a variety, not only live oaks, but also swamp maple trees, dogwoods, azaleas, camellias, white wisteria and irises."

His wife, the late Jimmy Lea, and he bought the land from Fred Fenn, an LSU dean. "We got the land in 1961 and built our house in 1965," he stated. "It was well developed out here when we built but we had no entry off of Kimbro and had to make one."

Clifford and Ruth Comeaux Babin, along with Moles, participated in the citizens' patrol for Magnolia Woods. Their small, secluded-by-shrubbery house on Kimbro Drive is sited on a large lot. They like the natural look and the trees, including oak, pine, ironwood and cottonwood. They bought their lot from Lea in December 1955, built the first part of the house in 1956 and moved into their home in April 1956.

Lea constructed Laurel Lea Shopping Center at Highland Road and Staring Lane about 1956, later selling it. Gene Rozas, who leased it, said he has seen phenomenal growth in the area. "When I started working here, Kenilworth and the Gardere Lane area were not here. I remembered the farmland below Highland Road that was considered a natural levee for the Mississippi. People did not build below Highland Road."

Subdivision restrictions signed June 22, 1953, specify that no dwelling shall be permitted on any lot at a cost of less than $8,000 and houses were subject to approval of an architectural control committee. Also: "No noxious or offensive activities shall be carried on upon any lot nor should anything be done thereon which may or may not become an annoyance or nuisance to the neighborhood." As for livestock, only chickens for personal use, horses and pets were allowed. The only garage apartments permitted were for domestic services, and no one could occupy a house until the exterior had been finished. Furthermore: "No tourist court, gambling establishment, barroom, saloon or other establishment intended primarily for the retail salt of malt, spirituous or vinous liquers, shall be constructed, operated or permitted to remain on these premises."

Integrated and Friendly: South Highlands

When South Highlands subdivision was developed by the late Durward Gully of Gully and Associates, in three filings off Staring Lane from 1968 to 1973, it was outside the city limits, but early residents believed the city would grow in that direction. They were right. "We had to call the sheriff's office for everything when I first moved here," said Theresa Johnson Blount, who has lived here with her family since 1978.

Gully, who bought a wealth of acreage and filed for subdivisions across the area, built most of the brick and brick-veneer houses, the majority with three or four bedrooms and two baths. He purchased some land from the heirs of Dr. Houston Staring, a son of merchant-planter Joe Staring, who had property referred to as Bellonia and Doolitle Plantations. "Houston Staring was a prominent citizen with a store at Burtville and several other properties, including a store at the end of Gardere Lane," according to a descendant, Lucy Staring Pope.

Entered via High Point Road, it dead-ends at the rear at Raintree Road. Like many other subdivisions, it was built from back to front. The boundaries are Staring, Raintree, Nolen and Windward Roads and part of Halfway Tree, Rustwood and Wild Valley Roads.

Integrated from the outset, South Highlands remains a friendly, integrated and quiet neighborhood, predominantly African American. Some 150 homeowners work together through the South Highlands Civic Association, founded by Victoria "Vickie" Lorraine in 1976. She initiated cash stipends to high school and college graduates, prepared Thanksgiving baskets for the needy and made sure that Christmas was celebrated in a big way.

Lemar Proctor, a retired principal, has lived here with his wife, Doris, since 1977 and served as association treasurer. "We're at the front of the subdivision and bought before it was built," he said. "I came to a meeting at the school and saw the For Sale sign and the slab was down. We selected the colors."

Wildwood Elementary School, built in 1969 when students were mandated to live within the school district, was a drawing card for many residents.

"We moved here in 1980 when Dick got a job teaching at LSU," said Jean Bengtsen. "It was close to campus and both children went to Wildwood Elementary, right here." When they house shopped, it was between Christmas and New Year's, she said. "I saw wooden yard signs bearing the family's name at every house. I was impressed with how 'gung ho' the neighborhood was."

Another past association president, Isadore A. Brown Jr., said that he and his wife, Barbara, moved from North Baton Rouge for the school for their three children, the sidewalks and closer distance to his work in Geismar. Among residents on the Wildwood Elementary School faculty were Aubrey Burrell and Ellis Thomas, the latter serving as newsletter editor and updating the residential list.

Bluebonnet Boulevard

Fly-In Guests Welcomed

Residents of Woodlake at Bluebonnet subdivision are happily aware of their prized location adjacent to the 101-acre Bluebonnet Nature Preserve and Swamp. In the midst of city life, they have two lakes and sixty-plus homes on 75 acres. Sited on the edge of the 250-year-old cypress and tupelo Bluebonnet Swamp brings them bountiful wildlife and fly-in guests from the crane family.

"We love this setting," said Allen Broyles, research associate at the LSU Ag Center's Burden Center. "The streets were still dirt roads in November 1992, when Nancy and I had the foundation laid, the first in the subdivision, and in March 1993, we moved in."

Developed by David Vey and Rick Hartley, the subdivision off Bluebonnet Boulevard has homes that are tastefully congruent in design and sited on spacious lots, the smallest of which is 90 by 150 feet. Timberlake Drive, the only entrance and exit, is a long curve around the lake, lending seclusion to the subdivision. Yet it is accessible to Interstates 10 and 12, historic Highland Road, the Mall of Louisiana and the picturesque Bluebonnet branch of the East Baton Rouge Parish Library, with its swampland boardwalks and hiking trails for the community.

"This was vacant, undeveloped land," said Vey. "Property owners adjacent to the lakes maintain them. All of the property on Bluebonnet was an assemblage of property owned by the American Bank and the Resolution Trust Corp."

Environmentalists, including Claire Coco, director of BREC's Bluebonnet Swamp Nature Center, hailed the rescue of the land and expressed gratitude to the developers and all who work to preserve presentation of the historic area.

In 1980, Bluebonnet Boulevard was built, and its first commercial building followed in 1981. The subdivision has a civic association, led by Gus Kousoulas, and residents abide by stringent restrictions, from mailbox design to lighting and landscaping.

Allen and Nancy Broyles co-chaired the landscape committee, and Allen landscaped his lot. Louisiana master gardeners through the LSU Cooperative Extension agriculture program, they lavishly plant their lawn with perennial and annual plants. One year they had an Improved Blaze Rose Bush that had more than five hundred blooms.

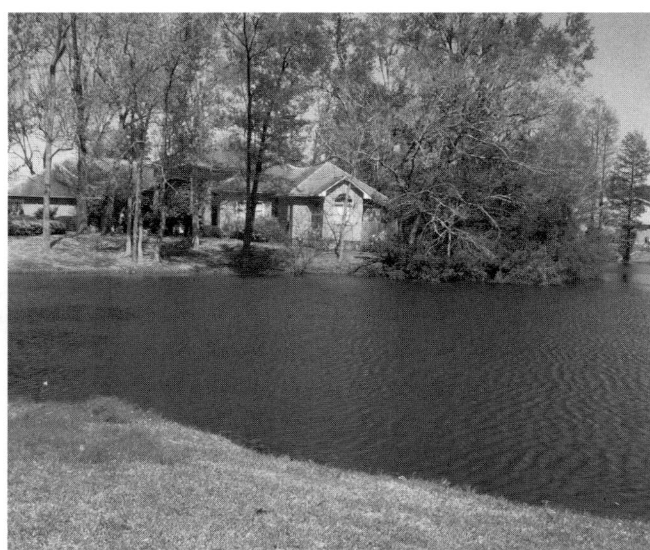

James and Jeannie LeFebvre, from their home on a mini peninsula in Wood Lake near Bluebonnet Swamp, have spectacular views. *Photo by Jeannie LeFebvre.*

Among the rare settings is that of James and Jeannie LeFebvre, who own a Floridian-style brick and stucco house exceeding four thousand square feet on Wood Lake. "We like living on a mini-peninsula surrounded by water," said Jeannie. "Our driveway goes through Wood Lake." After they bought their house in 2001, they gutted it and made major renovations, doing much of the work themselves. The home has spectacular views and is ideal for a couple that entertains. They can sit outside on a covered marble patio watching koi in a pool or swim in their free-form pool.

Kousoulas recalled that only half a dozen houses had been built when he and his wife, Effie, moved into their Vieux Carre–style brick and stucco two-story house. "For two years, the first residents worked with the developers on the front entrance and grounds," he noted.

How many subdivisions have their own castle? A home with a medieval feeling that resembles a castle is owned by Martin and Debbie Marchiafava. Martin, who belonged to the Society for Creative Anachronism, spent two years designing the house with a tower. A suit of armor is one personal touch in the Gothic-flavor two-story home. Inside, accoutrements include a spiral staircase, three fireplaces, stained concrete flooring, handmade windows and detailed woodworking. On Halloween, the parents of three children know how to make it spooky, and the setting lends itself to the neighbors' enjoyment. All that is lacking is a moat out front.

Lagniappe

Plantation Era Remembered: Riverbend, Riverbend Landing

Riverbend subdivision, located off Brightside Lane south of LSU, carries its symbolic street signs and forested lots into the future like a serene and gracious link to the past. At the site where Hope Estate and Arlington Plantations existed through the Civil War era, the streets are named for plantation owners like Valcour Aime and for plantations like Tezcuco. As did the plantation dwellers, residents enjoy the breeze from the Mississippi River, music of riverboat foghorns and wildlife.

Will Ourso, son of the late Mr. and Mrs. Clifford Ourso and the original subdivision developer, lives on Belle Grove Avenue. "I'm steeped in the history of River Road and our area, and I love it," he said. "Over thirty years ago, I purchased Arlington from the late Senator J.E. Jumonville Sr. and Hope Estate from Jane Duplantier Kelley and her brother, the late D.A. Duplantier."

An A. Hays Town–designed entrance leads into the subdivision between River Road and Nicholson Drive. Ourso planned the layout. "At the time, Mr. Town was designing my new home off Highland Road, and we became friends," he said. "While visiting Europe one summer, he took a picture of the entrance to this big beautiful estate about forty miles out of Paris and drew it for me. He named the streets. There's a lot of history here."

In 1979, Ourso, who was the first to develop anything in the area, conferred with his engineers and contractors to start plans. "We began the

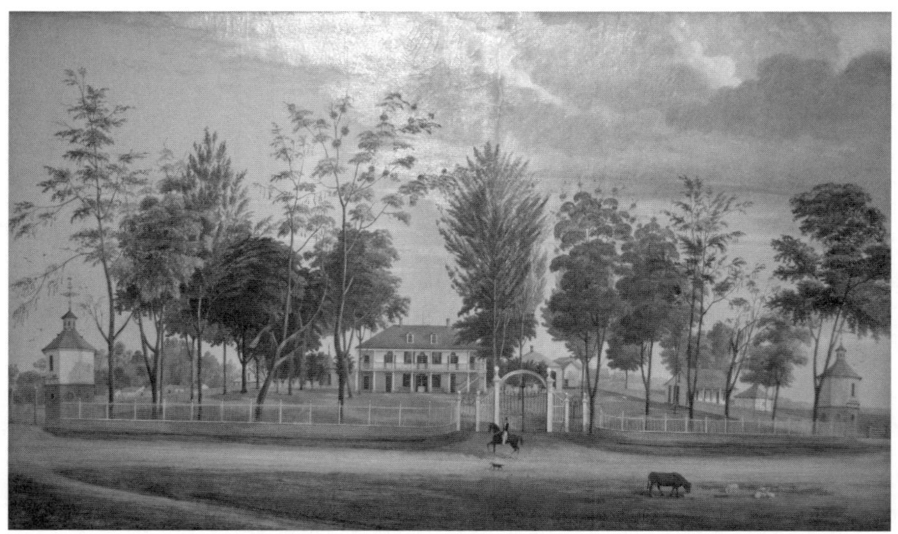

Riverbend is sited on land that was once pre–Civil War Hope Estate and Arlington Plantations. *Marie Persac,* Hope Estate Plantation, *LSU Museum of Art, Beth Ann Gold, photographer.*

boulevard first," he said. "We realized there was a housing need for people who work downtown and at the university. We have many state employees, including those at LSU, and lawyers, doctors and medical personnel. It's unbelievable the number of engineers and plant supervisors here."

Throughout Riverbend are unique, custom-built houses in varied architectural styles. Residing in their third home in Riverbend are attorney Murphy Foster III and his wife, Diane. "We built one of the first houses out here," said Murphy, son of former Governor and Mrs. Murphy Foster. "At the time, Diane and I did not know we could have children. In less than one year and a half after we moved here, Diane found out she was going to have a baby. We liked the house, but the floor plan was not feasible for a family. We built a larger, two-story house on a big treed lot. One day a realtor knocked on the door and said someone was interested in our house and would make it worth our while." He said they ended up selling it and building a similar house around the corner.

Diane, who drew floor plans for both houses, said, "My ideas came from the house where Murphy grew up in Franklin, once used as an orphanage," she said. "I like a lot of color in the furnishings." The house has warmth with bricks, wood floors and cypress and French and English furnishings.

A Williamsburg house nestled between three large oaks trees was a dream come true for Michael and Pam Wall on Belle Cherie Avenue. "We wanted a Williamsburg home," said Pam. "We designed the house and knew the dimensions before we bought the lot, then we came out and decided where we wanted the house situated." Wall, a chemical engineer who enjoys refinishing antiques, also wanted a workshop.

When they built their house in 1980, not many people were building houses on piers. They found a builder, P.A. Cherry, who was enthusiastic about doing something different. Made of taupe clapboard, neat with dark red shutters, the house lends itself to its interior furnishings. "We bought our flooring from salvage from the old Kansas City Southern and Louisiana and Arkansas Railroad, located on Fourteenth Street, just off Government Street. The walls and ceilings of the depot were used for our walls."

The history is apparent in the homes and in the activities. The subdivision's newsletter, *The Link*, edited by Adrienne Bowser, is an appropriate name, since Riverbend is like a family and the neighborhood also represents a link to plantation life history. A strong homeowners' association has annual dues that pay for security police patrols and two major social outings a year. Riverbend has over 450 families, excluding the pocket subdivision Riverbend Lakes, which has its own civic association.

Once nineteenth-century Arlington Plantation, Riverbend Landing off Brightside Lane has some houses that back up to BREC's Farr Park on the River Road. An Old South flavor permeates the 114-home subdivision, one entrance closer to River Road than Riverbend.

"If you've seen those old maps, you know that the land from the river on back was one plantation after the other," said Ourso, also a Riverbend developer. "The first plantation south was Hope Estate, now Riverbend. A big canal exists where you enter Riverbend.

"When I bought Arlington over thirty years ago, it was raw land," said Ourso. "The forty acres that are Riverbend Landing were part of an original block of over five hundred acres I owned." In 1987, Ourso had the main boulevard, River Meadow Drive, constructed down the middle of Riverbend Landing. He put in the sewer system, built the entrance wall and donated land for Farr Park. Later, developers David Vey and Rick Hartley acquired the land and finished the development. Don Joffrion developed several filings and built seventy-six houses.

The spin-off streets from the long, meandering River Meadow Drive are cul-de-sacs and courts, reached only through one entrance-exit, River Meadow.

Veronica Winchester, president of the Riverbend Landing Homeowners' Association, continually works to have the separate filings function as one cohesive homeowners' group. She and her husband, Chad, like to garden in their fenced backyard on a 95- by 145-foot lot. She also cans their produce. The couple likes to entertain; at a joint birthday party in June for Chad and Tina Smith, a neighbor, Chad's band, Voodoo Chili, played.

"We love the view from our backyard," said Dr. Gary Wise of LSU on Riverway Drive. "We can see the trees of Farr Park and we have a canal—a great place to watch birds, see turtles, nutria, gar and wood ducks. We have a birdfeeder and see indigo bunting and other exotic birds."

When they moved onto River Meadow Drive, Alyce Lappin and Steve Jungk wanted a dog and needed more room, says Alyce. They built on a pie-shaped lot more than two hundred square feet deep. They like gardening and cooking and fenced a yard for their German shepherd, Rick.

Katie Gunn and Carolyn Ray are walking buddies, accompanied by Katie's dog Lacy, a white spitz. They like the sidewalks and chatting with neighbors. More pet lovers, Dr. and Mrs. Ronald "Ron" Malone, LSU, at 3218 Riverwalk Drive, and family enjoy their large home designed for entertaining, a lot just under an acre and their Jack Russell terrier, Toby, and their golden retriever, Rusty.

Another LSU faculty member, David Kurpius, lives with his wife, Allison, and two sons on Riverbrook Court. Their brick and stucco home is sited on a large, pie-shaped lot with space for the boys to play ball and have a playground area. Vice-president of landscaping, Kurpius says, "We're planting new trees this fall." For three years the Kurpiuses gave a fall party for the neighborhood.

Riverbend Landing attracts retirees. The homes are occupied by culturally diverse, educated professionals.

About the Author

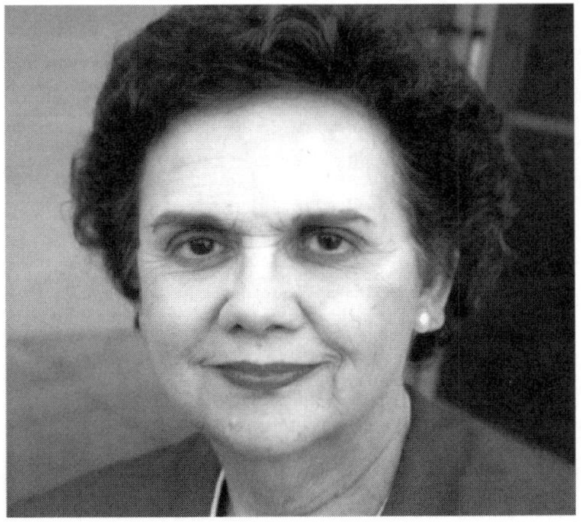

Photo by Ashley Armstrong.

Since she was sixteen, Annabelle Armstrong has been writing for newspapers, first in her hometown of Greenville, Mississippi, with the renowned publisher-editor Hodding Carter Jr. and later with the *Advocate* in Baton Rouge. After taking early retirement in 1986, she began writing across the area as a freelancer. In her sixth decade of journalism, a resident of Baton Rouge who has earned numerous journalistic awards, she continues to share subjects and sites with readers. A graduate of Southeastern Louisiana University and recipient of its Alumni Distinguished Service Award, she works part time at the Louisiana State Archives. She is deeply grateful to her son, Kenny, and daughter, Delma, and for countless neighborhood leaders and historians for assisting with this project.